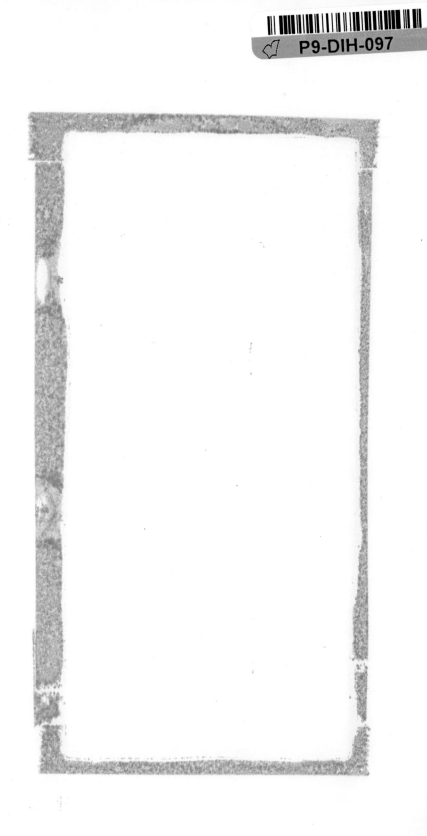

Depression: Its Diagnosis and Treatment
Lithium: The History of its Use in Psychiatry

Depression: Its Diagnosis and Treatment

Lithium:
The History of its Use in Psychiatry

By Nathan S. Kline

State of New York
Department of Mental Hygiene
Rockland State Hospital
Orangeburg, N.Y.

With 14 tables

BRUNNER/MAZEL *Publishers* • New York

The original edition of this volume was published as Vol. 3
of the series *Modern Problems of Pharmacopsychiatry*

Copyright © 1969 by S. Karger, AG, Basel, Switzerland

Published by
BRUNNER/MAZEL, INC.
80 East 11th Street
New York, N.Y. 10003

Library of Congress Catalog Card No. 74-108115

SBN 87630-023-9

Manufactured in the United States of America

Index

Preface

The pharmaceutical treatment of depression has raised at least as many questions as it has answered. The very success of the treatment has led to serious doubts about accepted methods of classification and accepted theories of etiology.

It must be remembered that these drugs are called 'antidepressants' only because we so designate them. In their ignorance of the semantic limitation we have placed on them they may nevertheless go ahead and provide effective treatment for a variety of other conditions such as some of the anxieties, phobias, obsessions and disturbed states of childhood and adolescence. We are then faced with a dilemma: either the drugs are useful for conditions other than depression or certain other conditions are in reality depression-equivalents. My personal preference is for this latter view but the former is certainly a defensible position.

To further complicate the picture, until quite recently one of the largest selling preparations for the treatment of depression was Deprol (a combination of meprobamate and benactyzine). In the drug underground benactyzine is one of the substances referred to as HOG which is used in a manner similar to LSD for its dissociating and perception distorting properties. This mode of relief of depression is probably similar to that of Ditran (N-ethyl-3-piperidyl cyclopentyl-phenylglycolate HCl) which had a short-lived fame as a 'single shot' treatment of depression. The treatment worked so long as the dissociation persisted but returned in most cases when the personality began to reintegrate.

There is also a body of both opinion and evidence that phenothiazines and phenothiazine-like preparations such as thioridazine (Mellaril) or thioxanthenes, such as thiothixene (Navane), are also effective in the treatment of depression. Whether these depressions are different from the ones which respond to antidepressant medications is as yet unclear. Perhaps these drugs have also been mislabeled or perhaps, more fundamentally, our categoric conceptualization of the whole field of mental illness is irrelevant from the pharmaceutical point of view.

With full knowledge of these limitations I have heuristically classified those conditions commonly collected under the rubric of depression and described their treatment with those preparations which we presently label as antidepressants. As a researcher it is evident that the nature of depression, its etiology, its diagnosis, its physical concomitants, and the reasons for success of pharmaceutical treatment are far from known. Two-thirds of my professional life is spent directly or indirectly in the exhilarating, although often frustrating, pursuit of answers to these questions. The other one-third of my time involves the treatment of 400 to 500 new patients each year and the continuing care of many more. Over 70% of these patients seen in private practice suffer from depression. Suffer is often too mild a term for the wracking agony and raw pain which cries out for relief. Despite the limitations of knowledge it is the glory of the physician that he learns as much as he can from books, journals, lectures, his colleagues and particularly from his own experience; that he apply this knowledge with all the skill and care of which he is capable, knowing he can influence but not command nature. It is hoped that the present volume will contribute to this end.

Depression: Its Diagnosis and Treatment

'Puella Nigersis ridebat
Quam tigris in tergo vehebat;
Externa profecta
Interna revecta
Sed risus cum tigre manebat'

Genius is usually referred to as 'brooding and melancholy' whereas it is the moron who is 'happy'. What a commentary upon the values and achievements of 7,000 years of human civilization! BURTON'S *Anatomy of Melancholy* even after the passage of more than 300 years appears likely to be one of the most enduring books in the English language. The illustrious SAMUEL JOHNSON remarked to BOSWELL that it was the only book that ever got him out of bed 'two hours sooner than he wished to rise' [9].

A.   The Four Psychiatric Uses of the Term 'Depression'

1.   Existential Depression

Depression is a condition of existence. The pleasures of acquisition, achievement and unexpected good fortune are balanced by the sorrows of loss, failure and undeserved bad luck so that depression is part of the human condition. Environmental extremes (including unrelieved uniformity) may result in a similar response. The intensity of this 'existential depression' is also determined by less personal realities (war, economic depression, national disgrace or their equivalents), by the spirit or fashion of the times (eighteenth century melancholia, nineteenth century *Weltschmerz* or contemporary Cool) and finally by individual personal disposition and temperament.

Were there no such thing as depression we would lack much of the world's great tragic literature, music and art. Without such depression we would be less than, or at any rate other than, human.

2.   Secondary Symptomatic Depression

When depression possesses a special quality or is of inappropriate intensity or duration it ceases to be merely an existential condition and must be regarded as a symptom.

a)   From drug sedation

Among the most common causes of such depressive symptoms is medication. Reserpine is one of the few drugs which has been identified as sometimes having such a side effect. Curiously in the case of reserpine, depression may not be due to any direct action but may arise secondarily since a certain type of driving, overexerting individual with a need to prove his or her potency in life often tends to develop vascular hypertension. Add to this the fact that reserpine is a sedative and anything which interferes with the capacity to demonstrate and experience this feeling of power is likely to induce depression. Before the days of reserpine the same depressions were sometimes produced by barbiturates, bromides or even enforced bed rest.

b)   From other drug action

There are, however, depressions which seem more definitely related to drugs such as corticosteroids (e. g. Cortisone) and certain sulfonamides such as methenamine mandelate (Mandelamine). Possibly a number of the oral contraceptives may induce depression although satisfactory statistics are not yet available.

c)   From viral diseases

Almost any of the virus diseases have depression as a frequent accompaniment as well as a sequela. Anyone who has had infectious mononucleosis need not be reminded of this fact. Even common viral upper respiratory or gastrointestinal infections are apt to be followed by a month or two of mild depressive symptoms. Obviously it is important that both the therapist and the patient be aware of this in order not to misjudge the course of the disease or of the treatment.

d)   From operative procedures

Whether because of anesthesia, threat to the body image or some unidentified cause, there is no question but that postsurgical patients have a higher incidence of depression than would otherwise be expected. This occurs without regard to the success of the surgery or even the diagnosis (as for instance in those patients operated on for neoplasm in whom the condition proves to be benign).

e)   From parturition

Post-partum depressions as well as pre-menstrual depressions are so generally accepted as 'normal' that they are often not discussed. Until we know more of the biochemistry it is impossible to differentiate the psychological from the endocrinological factors possibly involved.

f)   From other physical conditions

A large variety of other physiological disorders may also be productive of depression. There is even evidence that races other than the French also suffer from depression because of liver disorders. Any physical disorder ranging from avitaminosis to brain tumor can contribute to or cause depression and such factors must be eliminated, or at least taken into account, before the depression can be regarded as other than secondary.

g)   From other psychological disorders

Similarly depression can be secondary to psychological states such as anxiety, schizophrenia or diseases of the senium. Our ignorance is sufficient to obscure differentiation of whether the origins are psychodynamic, physiological or both.

3.   The Depressive Syndrome

a)   Characteristics

In existential depression and in secondary symptomatic depression the major characteristic is a feeling tone of sadness, dejection and hopelessness. Although the differentiation is not absolute, when the degree of severity becomes sufficient and certain new features are added we tend to think of depression as more than a symptom, i.e., as a syndrome. Whether it is via extension of affect or of separate origin the thought and behavior of the patient also begin to show marked changes. In addition to the affective and thinking disorders there are also behavioral and physiological manifestations. Decreased interest in the environment and lessened social participation are common. Fatigue, disturbances of sleep and especially early morning insomnia are quite characteristic. Autonomic lability may produce otherwise unimportant physical manifestations which result in preoccupation with some body function or organ. Worries about heart disease, cancer and other dire disorders are prominent. Since decrease in appetite and weight loss are common, in the moderate cases there may be a 'sweet reasonableness' about these beliefs but on other occasions the rationale is so remote that it is outright irrational and delusional.

b)   *Unfortunate confusion with schizophrenia*

In certain types of depression a slowing of the intellectual process occurs and the distortions of thinking may extend to preoccupation with suicide, ideas of nihilism, delusions or even hallucinations. Unfortunately it is too often forgotten that delusions and hallucinations can be part of the depressive syndrome so that a misdiagnosis of schizo-affective disorder or even unqualified schizophrenia is sometimes routinely made if delusions and hallucinations are present. The misdiagnosis is reinforced by mistaking retardation for blocking. As a consequence antidepressant medications which would be highly effective are not only overlooked but are regarded as contraindicated.

c)   *Masking by anxiety*

At times the patient reacts with great concern to his retardation or to his nihilistic thoughts. He may then become so disturbed that the depression is overshadowed by anxiety. The same is true at the physiological-behavioral level so that occasionally agitation completely masks the retardation. Cases such as these may be misdiagnosed as anxiety states which is a serious error because although sedatives and related drugs used for treatment may dampen the anxiety or agitation they usually increase the depression still further.

4.   Depression as a Disease

a)   Basic and compensatory features

It is most unfortunate that the same word 'depression' is used for the existential state, the symptom, the syndrome and the disease entity. The first three uses all have in common the affective state which is conveyed by the common meaning of the term depression. Most psychiatrists are convinced that depression as a basic disease entity can manifest itself in a number of ways including some which do not include feelings of dejection or sadness. Semantic confusion is unavoidable when we begin talking about a depression 'without depression'.

In part the expression and manifestations of the depression are dependent upon both the culture and the personality structure of the individual patient. As I have discussed at some length elsewhere [12, 15] there exists not only a basic disorder (such as depression) which is relatively fixed and universal but there are also compensatory reactions to the basic disorder (roughly analogous to compensatory emphysema) and these are indeed modifiable.

b)   Cultural influences

In general those cultures which place a high value on both the privileges and responsibilities of the individual produce depressions characterized by feelings of guilt, alienation and hopelessness. The West (with its Judeo-Christian ethic) leads to such reactions which can become so severe that escape by suicide seems to the sufferer as the only possible solution.

By way of contrast those societies in which the individual is de-emphasized in favor of the extended family or some type of tribe identification rarely lead to feelings of isolation, hopelessness or guilt. Thus suicide in Indonesia, for instance, is almost unknown in those parts of the country where native non-Western values still prevail. In these regions as a rule depression manifests itself largely in a psychosomatic form or as a paranoid confusional state.

c)   Depression equivalents (psychosomatic, phobic-obsessive, addictive)

There has been increasing recognition in our own culture that depression has many more equivalents than was formerly believed to be the case. The evidence that depression in much of Asia and Africa is expressed through somatic symptoms has led us to examine whether this may not also be true in our own culture. The belief that psychosomatic disorders are primarily a sublimation of anxiety must be reappraised. Further, a strong case can be made for the fact that some of the phobic and obsessive compulsive disorders are techniques for shortcircuiting depression [11]. Our work in Iran [18, 19] has demonstrated that depression underlies some instances of narcotic addiction as may also be the case with alcoholism and other types of drug abuse.

d)   Historical perspective of drug abuse

Widespread indulgence in and acceptance of disinhibiting drugs such as alcohol and barbiturates, stimulating preparations such as caffeine and amphetamines, and dissociating drugs such as marijuana and LSD appear to parallel existential depression, anxiety and lack of orientation of a particular society at a particular time [14]. There is historical evidence for this. The Soma referred to in the Rig-Veda may well have been the hallucinogen amanita muscaria [25] and similar substances were probably still in use a few thousand years later in conjunction with both the Orphic and Eleusinian Mysteries. The dancing mania of The Middle Age was in part associated with ergot; during the witches' Sabbaths, candles containing psychoactive substances were burned [2]. The more recent nineteeth century epidemic of cocaine usage is also compatible with this hypothesis. At a contemporary cross-cultural level the acceptability of opium, hashish and kat in certain countries are further instances.

e)   Other depression equivalents (pseudo-senility, anxiety, social maladaptation)

The availability of treatment techniques has led us to examine more closely whether depression does not manifest itself in yet other ways.

Therapeutic trials have demonstrated that some instances of presumed cerebral arteriosclerosis or senility were reversed by antidepressant medications. Since there is no real reason to believe that any of the antidepressant drugs affect the arteriosclerotic or the senile process we can only assume that these were cases of pseudo-arteriosclerotic and pseudo-senile deterioration.

It is less clear whether those cases of anxiety which respond to antidepressant medications are really covert depressions or whether the medications used are also effective agents against anxiety. The fact that we call these medications 'antidepressants' does not limit their range of therapeutic action and perhaps we are incorrect in designating them by such a narrow term.

The chronically fatigued and bored as well as the underachievers may in actuality be victims of previously unrecognized forms of depression. Even more intriguing is the possibility that the hyperkinetic child may be compensating for an underlying depression. This would explain the otherwise almost contradictory finding that amphetamines are therapeutically effective. Some rebellious and delinquent adolescent behavior may also be a compensation for depression and, although I have not conducted a formal study, there is no question that a gratifyingly high percentage of such patients whom I treat with antidepressants have been relieved (as have their families).

B. Classifications of Depression

In its classic form depression is manifest by feelings of sadness, fatigue, loss of interest in the social environment, self neglect, insomnia, and fear of the patient that the condition is permanent and untreatable. In addition tearfulness, irritability, apathy, feelings of guilt, anorexia, constipation, loss of libido and depersonalization, nihilistic or suicidal preoccupation are some of the other characteristics which may or may not be present. Attempts have been made to classify depressions based on these symptoms as well as whether there is a family history of similar disorders, whether the depression is worse at a particular time of day, whether there have been previous depressions or manic states, relationship to menopause or childbearing, and the presence or absence of environmental circumstances which might have justified the depression.

A slight modification of the brilliant analysis of this problem by LEHMANN [26] can be outlined as follows:

1. Etiological Approach to Depression

    a) Endogenous vs reactive
    b) Toxic vs cultural-environmental

2. Taxonomic Approach to Depression

a) Historical

   I. Single episode
   II. Recurrent depression
   III. Manic depressive

b) Descriptive

   I. Agitated
   II. Retarded
   III. Paranoid

3.   Inferential Approach to Depression

a) Psychodynamic

   I. Aggression turned inward
   II. Libidinal cathexis
   III. Psychic mourning
   IV. Other

b) Physiological

   I. Disordered membrane permeability at the synapses
   II. Deficiency of free amines at the nerve endings
   III. Lack of stimulation of the pleasure or reward center
   IV. Other

4.   Experimental Approach to Depression

a) Electroencephalographic patterning

b) Autonomic responsivity
c) Endocrine typology
d) Conditioned responsivity
e) Pharmacological reactivity

5.   Observational Approach to Depression

a) Factor or principal component analysis of symptoms
b) Identification of subgroups within the population based on physiological-psychological characteristics

It should be emphasized that whereas the above categorization follows the overall analysis of approaches of LEHMANN, the specific subcategories have been modified in a manner to make them compatible with my own convictions and prejudices. At best this brief summarization is a poor substitute for the original. Reading of the full text by LEHMANN is recommended.

C.   The Relationship of Classification to Treatment

Almost all the literature dealing with pharmacotherapy compares the value of the two major types of pharmaceuticals, the tricyclics and the monamine oxidase inhibitors, in terms of how effective they are against Endogenous depressions as opposed to Reactive depressions. The seemingly simple question of determining which group of drugs is effective against which type of depression is in large part unanswerable because it is really unaskable.

1.   Monamine Oxidase Inhibitors (MAOIs)

Pharmacologically the monamine oxidase inhibitors are so called because all of them inhibit the enzyme which is necessary for oxidation of a particular group of amines. Hundreds of such preparations have been tested in the laboratory but the ability of a particular preparation to inhibit amines in vitro unfortunately has not provided an index of how effective it is likely to be against depression *in vivo*. Further, there is not necessarily a similarity in chemical structure of those half dozen preparations (among the dozens tested clinically) which proved effective enough to be marketed.

2.   Tricyclics

On the other hand, the tricyclics were so named because of the occurrence of three contiguous benzene rings. Substitution of various elements and the addition of side chains have greatly modified the appearance of the first few active preparations but nevertheless enough similarity remains to retain the term tricyclic. Initially the mode of action was completely obscure and about the only thing that the drugs seemed to have in common was that they were *not* monamine oxidase inhibitors. Subsequent evidence points to the likelihood that by blocking the reuptake of amines they in turn produce an end result similar to the monamine oxidase inhibitors, i.e., both of them increase the quantity of free amines at the nerve endings.

3.   Relationship of Drug Efficacy to Type of Depression

If it is true that the pharmacological activity of these two different groups of drugs is based on their common ability to produce more free amines at the nerve endings we are immediately faced with a dilemma as to why there should be any difference in their effectiveness in Reactive as opposed to Endogenous depression. It would be easier to comprehend if Endogenous depressions responded better to pharmacotherapy than did Reactive depressions (or vice versa). However, for one drug to work better on Reactive and the other on Endogenous depressions would imply that in one type of depression amine oxidase inhibition was defective whereas in the other type the etiology was probably due to disorder of membrane permeability. Evidence of such a difference should ultimately be testable at the physiological or biochemical level. If true, it could lead to a badly needed technique for identifying the type and quantifying the degree of depression as well as making available a technique for new drug screening and a method of specifying probable effectiveness of a particular drug in a particular patient.

In addition to the confusion resulting from the fact that one group of pharmacological agents is based on their ability to inhibit monamine oxidase and the other is identified by a general type of chemical structure, we also have the problem of separating the Endogenous from the Reactive depressions. There has been a general increase in patients diagnosed as depressed. Whether this is due to an increase in depression or a shift in diagnostic criteria is not entirely clear. The change is not limited to the United States or Western Europe since SNEZHNEVSKY [24] has reported the same trend in the Soviet Union (along with a disappearance of catatonia similar to the decrease in the United States). Even within the past twenty years a remarkable change in statistics of the sub-types of depression has occurred. In contrast to the late 1940s there are today only one-third as many patients diagnosed as Manic Depressive but ten times as many classified as Neurotic Depressions.

Despite elaborate checklists the differential diagnosis shows the highest interrater reliability when it is arrived at by 'global' impression rather than specific items. This, I believe, is due in large part to the inadequacy of mathematical statistical models to handle the problem of sub-populations. There is at least hope that this problem too will be resolved in the not too distant future. My purely clinical impression is that my own differential diagnosis between Reactive and other types of depression is more based upon the presence or absence of neurotic behavior than upon the characteristics of the depression itself. This at least raises a possibility that depression is a single entity which occurs in neurotic as well as non-neurotic individuals. The argument for existence of at least two types of depression is that the condition also occurs in a group of generally non-neurotic patients with a set of features not usually found in the neurotics: family history which reveals other members with similar disorders; prior episodes in the same patient also without sufficient environmental justification and spontaneous remissions with substantial intervals of perfectly normal behavior.

In addition to this breakdown into Endogenous or Primary depression (including manic depressive, post-partum, involutional and recurrent depressions) as opposed to Reactive (Neurotic) depressions there exist all the other possible classifications described above. There have been a number of attempts to demonstrate that one group of drugs is more effective against a particular type of depression than is the other. Some of the studies have shown statistically significant differences but unfortunately the correlations are not always in the same direction. Under an NIMH grant [4] we are currently preparing to analyze some 1,000 ambulatory patients with depression who have been seen over the past four years but unless, when this has been completed, the data show otherwise I will retain the clinical impression that no significant difference exists which can be related to the type of depression. I am, however, equally convinced that there are some patients in each sub-type who will respond to monamine oxidase inhibitors but not tricyclics, others who will respond to tricyclics but not monamine oxidase inhibitors, some who will respond to either type of drug, some who will respond only to a combination of the MAO inhibitors and tricyclics and some who will not respond to pharmacotherapy at all.

4.   Importance of Classification for Reasons Other Than Efficacy

If in reality there is no relationship of drug efficacy to sub-type of depression, is there any sense at all in wasting time in attempting a differential diagnosis? Even though the per cent favorable response to the two types of medication does not significantly differ in the various diagnostic categories there are other factors which make such a differential diagnosis very valuable. In a recently completed study [23] of 80 patients on protriptyline (Vivactil) we had several very interesting findings:

a)   Incidence of dropout

Dropouts in the first month of treatment were much higher among the Neurotic depressives than among the Endogenous depressions;

b)   Reasons for dropping out

Such dropouts in the Neurotic depressive group with only one exception were either because of greater severity, greater frequency or (most likely) a lesser capacity to tolerate side effects. Side effects were not an important reason for dropouts among the Endogenous depressions.

c)   Dropout time and ultimate response

Among the Neurotic depressives if there was not at least moderate improvement in the first two weeks it was extremely unlikely that the patient would ultimately respond to the drug in a satisfactory manner. In contrast quite a number of the Endogenous depressions who had shown little or no response at the end of two weeks did begin improving at a later date and eventually achieved complete remission.

If these data are confirmed in the larger series presently under analysis there are some important conclusions that can be drawn in respect to management and indications for medication.

D. Selection of Appropriate Medication

1. The Uses of Psychomotor Stimulants and Sedatives

The first decision to be made is whether any medication at all is indicated. In general no treatment is indicated for 'existential' depressions but there are exceptions. Normal but extreme grief or other extraordinary conditions may exist which justify active pharmacological intervention. Amphetamines and amphetamine-like substances alone or in combination with a sedative are the medications of choice. Similarly when the depression is a side effect of some other drug the obvious course of action is withdrawal or substitution of the offending agent but circumstances also do exist in which it is necessary to continue the other medication or in which the period before naturally occurring remission of the depression is so protracted as to require more rapid response. The same is true in respect to recovery from virus and other somatic disorders. In all of these cases the psychomotor stimulants are the pharmaceuticals of choice and only if they prove unsuccessful would there be reason to consider use of the tricyclics or MAO inhibitors.

2. The Role of Electroconvulsive Treatment

If the patient is acutely suicidal and adequate supervision cannot be provided the treatment of choice is electroconvulsive therapy in combination with an antidepressant. If there is reason to believe that the patient will not take prescribed medication, if there are no relatives or friends to adequately follow the course of the illness and check on medication, and if hospitalization is impossible or refused, then even though the patient is not acutely suicidal, the desirability of electroconvulsive therapy is enhanced. There are also some extraordinary circumstances such as the imperative for rapid response, even with the deficits (such as memory disturbance) which usually occur, that would also justify ECT as the treatment of first choice. In combination with the antidepressants usually 3 or 4 ECT are sufficient. Failure to respond at all to extensive pharmacotherapy may also be an indication for ECT but not as a rule before 6 months of drug treatment. In the overwhelming majority of cases pharmacotherapy is the treatment of first choice for therapeutic, economic and a variety of other reasons [13].

3.   First Consideration: Contraindications

Once it has been decided pharmacotherapy is in order consideration should first be given to contraindications to the two types of drugs.

a)   Factors against tricyclic usage

Cardiovascular disease, thrombophlebitis, hyperthyroidism or concurrent thyroid medications, a history of either glaucoma or presently increased intraocular pressure would each shift the choice away from a tricyclic.

b)   Factors against MAOI usage

The presence of a pheochromocytoma, chronic alcohol consumption, a liver disorder or the presence of hypotension would shift the choice away from an MAO inhibitor.

c)   *Factors against use of either tricyclics or MAOIs*

Any organic cerebral disorder should induce caution in use of either type drug. In general the use of any medication during the first trimester of pregnancy requires somewhat greater than usual justification.

4.   Considerations of Prior Treatment

Prior history of failure of response to several tricyclics (given in adequate doses for adequate periods of time) would strongly indicate a trial of an MAO inhibitor. Similarly, failure on several MAO inhibitors would suggest the use of a preparation from the group which had not been tried. If the patient has had a history of prior attacks with favorable response to a particular drug, this would normally be the medication with which to start. Unfortunately there is sometimes not so favorable a response on read-ministration. This is compensated for by the fact that a medication which may previously have been of no help at times is later fully effective. Patients who have failed on both types of drugs should be treated as though they were new patients except that the combination of an MAOI and a tricyclic should be tried after a single failure on each type of drug rather than as described below.

5.   Tricyclics

a)   *Reasons for selecting a particular tricyclic*

I.   Contraindications and prior responses

In the absence of contraindications and if there is not a history of recent failure of several of these preparations, a tricyclic is the medication of choice with which to begin because dietary restrictions and supervision in general is less demanding than with the MAO inhibitors.

The selection of the particular preparation is dependent upon the degree of sedation desired.

II.   Degree of sedation desired

In patients whose symptoms include anxiety a tricyclic which also has sedative properties is usually in order whereas patients with marked apathy and dullness usually require a stimulant-activating type of tricyclic.

III.   Occupational requirements

The reason for qualifying these choices is that despite the presence of anxiety the patient's occupation or habits may be such that sedation is undesirable or even dangerous.

IV.   Supervision required and available

In contrast, even if lethargy is present a sedating tricyclic may be preferred if there is inadequate supervision and considerable suicidal probability. A stimulant-activating preparation may be undesirable until the antidepressant activity is reasonably assured.

V.   Capacity to tolerate side effects

A further consideration to which reference has already been made is the capacity to tolerate side effects and obviously one should try to select a drug which the patient will not discontinue on his own for this reason.

Thus there are at least five factors to be considered and it would be most useful to have an even larger range of tricyclics available in order to be able to select the one which is most appropriate for a particular patient at a particular time.

b)   *Time lapse between use of a tricyclic and an MAOI*

If there is failure of response to adequate trials of two successive tricyclics the use of an MAOI is in order. There exist recommendations that two weeks be allowed to elapse between discontinuing a tricyclic and starting an MAOI. In our own experience we have never had difficulty when changing in this direction but now, more out of respect for the opinions of others than out of conviction born of experience, we usually allow a few days to elapse. To be on the safe side we then usually start the MAOI at one per day for three days and increase it by one every three days until the selected dose has been reached.

c)   Dose range and administration

It is convenient that we can generalize as to the sedative or stimulant characteristics as well as the incidence of side effects for each of the presently marketed preparations. However, it is equally inconvenient that these are only generalizations and it is impossible to accurately predict how any particular patient will respond to any particular drug. Thus, it is a good idea to clarify to the patient that a certain amount of trial and error is involved so that he is prepared for a change in medication should this be required because of side effects or lack of response. Preparation of the patient for taking medication is discussed subsequently.

The tricyclics (see table I) can be ranged in respect to their usual sedative-activating effects as follows:

Table I. Sedative qualities of tricyclics

Sedative	Non-sedative	Activating
amitriptyline (Elavil)	desipramine (Norpramin, Pertofrane)	protriptyline (Vivactil)
nortriptyline (Aventyl)	imipramine (Tofranil)	

A new effective sedative tricyclic, doxepin (Sinequan), will be marketed soon.

Desipramine has fewer side effects than imipramine. Nortriptyline (less sedative) has fewer side effects than amitriptyline.

The following table (see table II) contains recommended dosage schedules for patients of average weight in the 15–60 year age range. Above average weight may justify 4 times a day usage and markedly reduced weight or advanced years may indicate 2 times a day administration.

Table II. Recommended dose schedule for tricyclics

	Initial dose 3 × a day	Average dose 3 × a day	High dose 3 × a day	Maintenance dose 1 or 2 × a day
amitriptyline (Elavil)	25 mg	50 mg	100 mg	10–25 mg
desipramine (Norpramin, Pertofrane)	25 mg	50 mg	100 mg	25 mg
imipramine (Tofranil)	25 mg	50 mg	100 mg	10–25 mg
nortriptyline (Aventyl)	25 mg	50 mg	100 mg	10–25 mg
protriptyline (Vivactil)	5 mg	10 mg	20 mg	5–10 mg

Dosage schedule for doxepin (Sinequan) is similar to that of amitriptyline.

If the sedative properties of the tricyclic become a problem one excellent way of handling the matter is to give the entire dose at bedtime. This technique is particularly useful in patients suffering insomnia because it often supplements the effectiveness of an hypnotic or may even make it possible to eliminate ordinary sleeping medication. This would agree with the impression that the sedative effects of the tricyclic may be related to the time of administration and should be so spaced. Average doses of sedatives or psychomotor stimulants are compatible with the tricyclics and may be used to counteract side effects.

d)   How and when to increase the amount of medication

If the patient fails to show any improvement in two weeks the dosage should be doubled and, if there is no response by the end of four weeks, a second tricyclic should be substituted and similarly tried. If there is some response but not sufficient, usually the dose should be continued unchanged until there is either satisfactory remission or the patient's condition has plateaued for four weeks or longer. Increase of dose (eventually up to the maximum) is indicated if a plateau has lasted a month or more. One reason for earlier substitution of another member of the same group is that side effects turn out to be undesirably different or more marked than had been anticipated.

6.   Monamine Oxidase Inhibitors

a)   Selection, dose range and administration

The MAO inhibitors can be rated in terms of potency rather than sedative-activating characteristics. Nialamide (Niamid) and isocarboxazid (Marplan) even in quite high doses are usually weaker psychic energizers than phenelzine (Nardil) and tranylcypromine (Parnate). Pargyline (Eutonyl) is marketed for its antihypertensive action but it is also an effective anti-depressant. The most potent preparation is not always the most desirable and judgment must be made as to how much 'energizing' is needed. The general properties are not always fully predictive to a particular patient.

As with the tricyclics, the antidepressant activity is based on total daily dose so that actually once a day administration is adequate. Most patients (and doctors) are more satisfied when the total daily amount is given in divided doses (see table III). There is an as yet unconfirmed report that sensitivity to foods and drugs is greatest shortly after ingestion of the MAOI. If true, this would be an important factor in deciding the time of day when the MAOI should be taken.

Table III. Recommended dose schedule for MAO inhibitors

	Initial dose 2 × a day	Average dose 2 × a day	High dose 2 × a day	Maintenance dose 1 to 2 × a day
isocarboxazid (Marplan)	10 mg	20 mg	30 mg	10 mg
nialamide (Niamid)	100 mg	200 mg	300 mg	50 mg
pargyline (Eutonyl)	25 mg	50 mg	75 mg	10–25 mg
phenelzine (Nardil)	15 mg	30 mg	45 mg	15 mg
tranylcypromine (Parnate)	10 mg	20 mg	30 mg	10 mg

b)   Time lapse between an MAOI and a tricyclic

Occasionally and probably because of its persisting action there may be toxic reactions if a tricyclic is started too soon after discontinuance of an MAOI. The recommended wait is again two weeks although we have found 5–7 days usually sufficient if the tricyclic is begun at one a day for three days and increased by one only every three days.

7.   Combined MAOIs and Tricyclics

If after failure on two MAOIs following failure on two tricyclics and with (and often without) a history of unsatisfactory response to ECT, the possibility of combining tricyclics and MAOIs must be considered.

a)   Legal status

Combining of tricyclics and MAO inhibitors should be done with full awareness that it entails a legal risk regardless of the therapeutic urgency or efficacy. As former Commissioner JAMES GODDARD has written [10]:

'And, of course, a physician on his own responsibility may administer a drug for an unapproved use or increase or decrease the dose in caring for his own patients. If he does so, he should recognize that he is departing from the established safe and effective uses, and that he may become involved in a legal case where the final printed labeling can be offered and used as the only conditions for which the drug has been proved safe and effective.'

Since the combination of tricyclics and MAOIs is recommended against on the package inserts the physician who has exhausted other therapeutic measures must consider whether the needs of the patients or his own added legal safety should be given priority. Officially to legally administer such a combination would require the filing of an Investigation New Drug (IND) application with the Food and Drug Administration.

b)   Technique of administration

In our own use of this combination in several hundred patients we have found if the patient has not responded continuing the full dose of whichever MAOI he is on and adding a very small dose of tricyclic (for instance, 10 mg of imipramine or its equivalent) once a day will often rapidly produce a favorable response when other measures have failed. If necessary

50266

the dosage of the tricyclic can gradually be increased every week or two until the desired response is obtained. A most satisfying number of such patients respond who have failed on the various drugs given individually.

If the patient happens to be on a tricyclic the addition of a small dose of an MAOI (such as 25–50 mg of nialamide or its equivalent) will usually produce similar results. After a one or two week trial the dose can likewise be increased if needed. HORWITZ [8] has reported similar results.

8.   Combined Tricyclics and Phenothiazines

At the time of this writing the only combination on the market of tricyclic and phenothiazine as a single preparation is that of perphenazine and amitriptyline. The combinations are perphenazine 2 mg and amitriptyline 25 mg (Etrafon or Triavil 225), perphenazine 4 mg and amitriptyline 10 mg (Etrafon-A or Triavil 410) and perphenazine 4 mg and amitriptyline 25 mg (Etrafon-Forte or Triavil 425).

There is argument about the value of combining several drugs into a single capsule or tablet. In our own experience these have often proved extremely useful. There are for instance agitated patients who are basically depressed but desire to take only sedative drugs which will inhibit their activity. At the other extreme are agitated patients who seek out only the activating drugs and avoid phenothiazines which are necessary to prevent the possible development of a florid psychotic reaction. There are also patients who object to taking a large number of pills regardless of explanations concerning potency. For these and other reasons drug combinations are often most valuable.

Obviously if a single medication will do, this is usually preferable. If a finer adjustment is needed it is easy to add either more tricyclic or phenothiazine to the 'guaranteed' basic quantities.

9.   Combined MAOIs and Phenothiazines

The same arguments for the value of a combination with monamine oxidase inhibitor applies as in the case of the tricyclics. One such preparation made up of tranylcypromine (Parnate) 10 mg and trifluperazine (Stelazine) 1 mg was in extensive clinical trial in the United States at one time and is presently marketed in most countries of the world. This combination known as Parstelin appeared to be of use at least equal to that of the combination with the tricyclic but was withdrawn about the time that tranylcypromine (Parnate) was temporarily taken off the market.

10.   Combined Tricyclics and Sedatives

At times even the most sedative of the tricyclics is not sufficient and it is desirable to add an additional sedative. The same arguments in favor of fixed dosage can be used for such a combination. A number of these are either in clinical trial or under consideration and will probably be marketed within a year.

11.   New Tricyclics and MAOI Antidepressants

A number of the MAO inhibitors that are on the market in other countries such as mebanazine (Actomol) are still in clinical trial and appear to be at least equal to any of the others presently available. In addition it is possible that pargyline (Eutonyl) will be again actively investigated for its antidepressant action and possibly marketed for this purpose as well as for its antihypertensive action.

A number of new tricyclics such as the protriptyline (Vivactil) previously described have recently been marketed and others such as doxepin (Sinequan) appear to be extremely active and are under extensive investigation.

A number of other preparations of quite different chemical structure are also being investigated for their antidepressant activities and may open up new classes of drugs for therapeutic use.

12.   Lithium

The use of lithium salts for the treatment of manic states is now generally accepted. The largest series in the literature are by BAASTRUP and SCHOU [1], GERSHON *et al.* [6] and (unpublished as yet) our own series [16] of well over 300 patients. The evidence is now quite substantial that continuing use of lithium is quite effective in the majority of patients with manic depressive mood swings in preventing both the manic and the depressive phases. More controversial but also more exciting because of greater applicability is the use of lithium to prevent recurrent depressions. Our own data up to the present would indicate that there are definitely patients in whom lithium appears to bring about this effect, others in whom it has had no beneficial (and possibly an undesirable) action and the largest number about whom we have not yet been able to draw definite conclusions since several years are really necessary to evaluate results.

One of the problems seems to be that continuing usage of the drug is really required and there may still be episodes during the first six months to one year although they tend to be shorter and less severe.

E. Incompatible Medical Conditions, Medications and Foods

1. Tricyclics

a) *The FDA derived list of tricyclic incompatibilities is to be found in table IV.*

Table IV. Incompatible medical conditions and medications for tricyclics as derived from FDA approved package inserts (as of 1967)

	amitriptyline (Elavil)	desipramine (Norpramin, Pertofrane)	imipramine (Tofranil)	nortriptyline (Aventyl)
Medical Conditions				
Increased intraocular pressure (e. g. glaucoma)	++	++	++	++
Urinary retention	+	++		++
Hyperthyroidism		++	++	
Epilepsy		++		++
Cardiovascular disease		++	+	
Overactivity, overstimulation, agitation	+	+	*	
Pregnancy	?	?	?	
Patients under 12 years of age			?	
Medications				
MAO inhibitors	+++	+++	+++	+++
Thyroid medications		+	++	
Sympathomimetics (including amphetamines)		++		

+++	contraindicated
++	great caution indicated
+	caution indicated
*	implication of inclusion under other items
?	not recommended because information lacking

b)   *Criticism of stated tricyclic incompatibilities respecting medical conditions*

I.   Inconsistencies of listing of the different drugs

In view of the great similarity of action of the various tricyclics it is surprising that certain medical conditions are regarded as contraindications for one drug but not the others. In our experience the drug incompatibilities for the various tricyclics seem to be equivalent and should be so treated.

II.   Increased intraocular pressure (e. g. glaucoma)

Rather interestingly, worsening of glaucoma is not specifically listed as a side effect under any of the medications. Apparently the dangers of increased intraocular pressure are included in the statement that all the tricyclics have anticholinergic effects. We have seen fit to add this as a separate item because of its great importance. Until the matter of use in patients with glaucoma has been settled it is probably wise to avoid tricyclics except when an antidepressant is essential and contraindications for other drugs are even greater or need is imperative.

III.   Urinary retention

The problem of urinary retention is more important than table IV might indicate and it is recommended that the tricyclics be avoided in patients who have difficulty voiding. A history of enlarged prostate or repeated genito-urinary infection are also incompatibilities.

IV.   Hyperthyroidism

The evidence for incompatibility with hyperthyroidism (and thyroid medications) has not been particularly striking in our own experience.

V.   Epilepsy

In our experience all (not just some) of the tricyclics lower the seizure threshold and in such patients it is wise to increase the anticonvulsant medications or add one of them if seizures are precipitated.

VI.   Cardiovascular disease

The caution is so general as to be worthless except as the basis for a law suit. More to the point is that occasional irregularities of beat or tachycardia or hypertension or hypotension may occur but are usually mild and transient. Whether 'heart disease' constitutes an incompatibility is questionable.

VII.   Overactivity, overstimulation and agitation

This item is so general as to be not only worthless but definitely wrong. There are frequent occasions when agitation, overactivity and even overstimulation are an accompaniment of depression. It may be that a sedative (phenothiazine or other type) may be needed simultaneously with the antidepressant but certainly the generalization of incompatibility is incorrect.

VIII.   Pregnancy

We have had patients progress from conception to delivery without difficulty. Except for the general practice of avoiding all medication during the first trimester of pregnancy (unless strongly needed) there is no reason in our own experience to be overly cautious on this score.

IX.   Patients under 12 years of age

Finally there is a curious caution against use of imipramine in patients under 12 years of age although no mention has been made of the use of this or other tricyclics in the treatment of enuresis which is the implicit reason for the limitation. This will be discussed subsequently but there certainly is no concrete evidence of any great importance indicating the existence of such an incompatibility.

c)   *Criticism of stated incompatibilities respecting other medications*

I.   MAOIs

This has been previously discussed (D-7).

II.   Thyroid medications

This has been discussed above (E-1-b-IV).

III.   Sympathomimetics (including amphetamines)

We have seen no evidence that there is any incompatibility between the tricyclics and the amphetamines or other sympathomimetic amines at ordinary dose levels either in oral or parenteral form.

2.   MAOIs

a)   *FDA derived list of MAOI incompatible medical conditions*

Table V presents a list of incompatible medical conditions for MAOIs as derived from the FDA approved package insert. Although pargyline (Eutonyl) is not FDA approved for use in psychiatry, it is nevertheless an MAO inhibitor with antidepressant potency comparable to the others and is therefore included.

It is obvious that the contraindications for isocarboxazid (Marplan) and nialamide (Niamid) are less than for the others which is in conformity with the fact that they are less active.

b)   *Criticism of stated MAOI incompatibilities respecting medical conditions*

I.   Age (over 60)

In our experience we have had no difficulty with patients over 60 years of age if the initial dose is somewhat reduced. In view of the large

Table V. Incompatible medical conditions for MAO inhibitors as derived from FDA approved package inserts

	isocarboxazid (Marplan)	nialamide (Niamid)	phenelzine (Nardil)	tranylcypromine (Parnate)	pargyline (Eutonyl)
Age					
Patients over 60 years of age			+++	+++	
Patients under 12 years of age					?
Liver conditions					
Severe liver disease	+++		+++	+++	++
History of liver disease	+++		+++	+++	
Abnormal liver function tests	+		+++	+++	
Cardiovascular conditions					
Cardiovascular disease	+	++	+++	+++	++
Hypertension		++	+++	++	
Malignant hypertension					?
Hypotension				+	+
Overactive or overeating angina patient	+	+			++
Cerebrovascular defect (confirmed or suspected)			+++	+++	
Impaired renal function	+++	+		+	++
Pheochromocytoma			+++	+++	+++
History of headache			+++	+++	
Epilepsy	+	+	+	+	
Pregnancy (especially first trimester)	+		?	++	?
Lactation				+	
Overactivity, overstimulation, agitation	+			+++	++
Hyperthyroidism					+++
Tuberculosis (if isoniazid may be needed)		+++			
Debilitation			+++		

+++	contraindicated
++	great caution indicated
+	caution indicated
*	implication of inclusion under other items
?	not recommended because information lacking

number of patients over this age who become depressed a contraindication for the use of MAOIs would be to deprive many patients of needed treatment. The failure to treat pargyline in the same manner respecting an age limitation illustrates how whimsical this contraindication is.

II.   Age (under 12)

Similar lack of experience would suggest caution in patients 12 years of age or younger. There is not the background of experience with enuretics although there were no disturbing results or side effects with autistic children so treated.

III.   Liver conditions (severe liver disease)

The virtual elimination of MAO inhibitors for patients with any evidence of liver disorder past or present is an irresponsible prohibition. This attitude undoubtedly grew out of the iproniazid (Marsilid) experience but there are many who feel that the danger of liver impairment was grossly exaggerated, if it occurred at all. We have used a variety of the MAOIs in treating a substantial number of patients with past and present liver disorders and have had no problems. Obviously it is desirable in such patients to carry out liver function tests somewhat more frequently than usual in order to 'play it safe'. Even when this is done a problem also exists because in a substantial number of depressed patients one of the four liver function tests we carry out is somewhat elevated to begin with. If such patients failed to respond to tricyclics we have not regarded the abnormal liver function test as an absolute prohibition against use of these drugs. A definite change in more than one of the tests which persists upon repetition of the test would indicate the need for more caution and a close search for evidence of a clinical change.

IV.   Liver conditions (history of liver disease)

This has been previously discussed (E-2-b-III)

V.   Liver conditions (abnormal liver functions tests)

This has been previously discussed (E-2-b-III)

VI.   Cardiovascular conditions (cardiovascular disease)

Caution in respect to cardiovascular disease is obvious as it would be for any drug. If there is any report of dizziness, syncope, etc. blood pressure should be obtained sitting, standing and standing after three minutes. The recommendation against use of 'antidepressant' MAOIs in hypertension is a curious one since pargyline (Eutonyl) in contrast actually has FDA approval as a recommended use for the treatment of this condition. Too rapid drop of blood pressure is always a danger and hence dosage of the drug should be started lower and increased gradually.

For patients with both hypertension and depression, the MAOIs are usually the drugs of choice since reserpine in some cases may deepen the depression. Dosage should be initiated with a lower than usual amount to prevent any abrupt drop. In our own experience a combination of MAOIs with *oral* sympathomimetic amines (including amphetamines) is not contraindicated if also started at small doses. Obviously massive doses are to be avoided as would be true in any case.

Hypotension may be more of a problem but use of an MAOI should depend upon the patient's clinical condition and not simply on blood pressure readings since many patients function in a completely satisfactory manner with systolic blood pressures consistently below 100. In the majority of hypotensive patients the MAOIs do not cause any important drop in blood pressure and in a number the blood pressure actually rises to within normal limits.

The caution for the anginal patient is a wise one which should apply to all MAOIs and not just those derived from the FDA listing. The fact is that the pain is often reduced (or ignored) and while the medication allows the patient to function more freely, warning should be given to restrict activity in accord with cardiovascular capacity and functioning rather than being based on how the patient feels.

If cerebral vascular defect is meant to include cerebral arteriosclerosis then our own experience would be in disagreement with this as an incompatibility. Depressed patients with cerebral arteriosclerosis have generally responded quite well although again lower than usual doses may be used at the onset. This caution probably arose as a 'deduction' because of blood pressure rise with certain foods as is discussed below.

VII.   Cardiovascular conditions (hypertension)

This has been previously discussed (E-2-b-VI)

VIII.   Cardiovascular conditions (malignant hypertension)

This has been previously discussed (E-2-b-VI)

IX.   Cardiovascular conditions (hypotension)

This has been previously discussed (E-2-b-VI)

X.   Cardiovascular conditions (overactive or overeating angina patient)

This has been previously discussed (E-2-b-VI)

XI.   Cardiovascular conditions (cerebrovascular defect [confirmed or suspected])

This has been previously discussed (E-2-b-VI)

XII.   Impaired renal function

Caution for patients with impaired renal function does not appear to differ materially from other drug usage. It seems unjust to rule out possibly effective treatment of depressed patients because they have impaired renal function. Certainly dosage of all medications should be given with caution and frequent examination for possible toxicity is in order, but the prohibition should not be absolute.

XIII. Pheochromocytoma

Not having had experience with pheochromocytoma there nevertheless appears to be justification for exclusion of this medication.

XIV.   History of headache

Headache is such a frequent manifestation of depression that it would be artificially restricting the use of the drug to rule out patients with a history of this condition. Certainly if tumor, aneurysm, etc. is suspected it should be immediately investigated. In the absence of such evidence the prohibition is downright silly.

XV.   Epilepsy

The tendency to lower epileptic threshold seems somewhat *understated* and very often increase of anticonvulsive medication is in order.

XVI.   Pregnancy (especially first trimester)

In respect to pregnancy we have had patients on both tricyclics and MAO inhibitors from start to finish without difficulty but obviously if medication is not needed it should not be prescribed.

XVII. Lactation

A caution respecting lactation would appear to be based upon concern that the MAOI is transmitted through the milk to the infant. We have had nursing mothers on MAOIs without any reported difficulties but caution is possibly in order until more is known.

XVIII. Overactivity, overstimulation and agitation

The same comments apply as in respect to the tricyclics. Often these are conditions which would indicate rather than contraindicate the use of these drugs. It may be desirable to accompany them with phenothiazines or sedatives as described below.

XIX.   Hyperthyroidism

The incompatibility with hyperthyroidism seems, on the other hand, somewhat understated since in general results with such patients have been far from satisfactory and sometimes the course is not too smooth. The recommendation is that if an MAOI is otherwise indicated that it be given but the patient followed more closely than would otherwise be necessary.

Table VI. Incompatible medications and foods for MAO inhibitors as derived from FDA approved package inserts

	isocarboxazid (Marplan)	nialamide (Niamid)	phenelzine (Nardil)	tranylcypromine (Parnate)	pargyline (Eutonyl)
Other MAOI	+++		+++	+++	++
Tricyclics (dibenzazepine derivatives)	+++	+	+++	+++	++
Phenylephrine (e. g. neo-synephrine)	++		+++	+++	++
Insulin	++				
Other psychotropic agents (e. g. sedatives)	++			+++	++
Alcohol	++	+	+++	+++	++
Opiates	++		+++	+++	++
Meperidine (Demerol)	++		+++	*	+++
Cocaine, Procaine and related preparations	++			*	
Antihypertensive agents	++		+++	+++	*
Parenteral guanethidine			*	*	++
Anesthetics (especially ether)	++			+++	++
Cheese	+		+++	+++	++
Pickled herring	+		+++	+++	*
Chianti, beer, yeast extract	*		+++	+++	*
Chicken liver	*		+++	+++	*
Pods of broad beans	*		+++	+++	*
Canned figs	*		*	+++	*
Reserpine		+		+++	
Antihistaminics	++			+++	++
Diuretics		++		+++	
Dopa, dopamine, tryptophane			+++	+++	++
Antiparkinsonian agents			++	++	
Over-the-counter drugs (for colds, hay fever, weight reduction)	*		+++	+++	++
Sympathomimetics (including amphetamines)			+++	+++	++
Parenteral reserpine					++
Caffeine					+

+++	contraindicated
++	great caution indicated
+	caution indicated
*	implication of inclusion under other items
?	not recommended because information lacking

XX.   Tuberculosis (if isoniazid may be needed)

We have had no experience with tubercular patients and whether MAOIs desensitize the patient for subsequent treatment with isoniazid seems an unsettled question. Certainly tricyclics would appear to be more than even ordinarily the drugs of first choice.

XXI.   Debilitation

The medication is of use in anorexic patients and, although a smaller dose than usual is indicated, there is no reason for ruling out its application. This is particularly true since one of the indications for MAOIs would appear to be anorexia nervosa.

c)   *FDA derived list of MAOI incompatible medications and foods*

The foods and medications stated to be incompatible with MAOIs are listed in table VI. These are derived from the FDA approved package inserts.

d)   *Criticism of stated MAOI incompatibilities respecting medications and foods*

I.   Other MAOIs

Contrary to the recommendations on the package inserts we have never had any difficulties arising as a result of combining various MAOIs with each other.

II.   Tricyclics

The combination of MAOIs and tricyclics has been discussed (D-7).

III.   Phenylephrine e.g. neo-synephrine, sympathomimetics (including amphetamines), etc.

Ordinary doses of *oral* sympathomimetics (including amphetamines) have not caused any difficulties. This definitely does *not* apply to the *paren-*

teral sympathomimetics which should be stringently avoided. If by mistake they are given then phentolamine methanesulfonate (Regitine) is extremely effective in averting or reducing the hypertensive response which might otherwise be quite dangerous.

Various types of decongestants such as used in many nose drops and in some over-the-counter preparations are potentiated in occasional patients. If they cannot be avoided, doses of one-quarter to one-third of the usual dose are often sufficient. It is almost impossible to prevent all patients from using these over-the-counter medications although recommendation against such usage is contained in the pamphlet of instructions 'So You Have A Depression' [17] given to each patient. A revision of this is included at the end of this paper. We do insist that patients phone or inquire about the use of over-the-counter preparations which at least serves to warn them to use such drugs cautiously. As a rule reduced amounts of such preparations are satisfactorily tolerated.

IV.   Insulin

We have had diabetics whom we have successfully treated with MAOIs while they were on insulin. The one major caution would seem to be that MAOIs can artificially depress blood sugar levels and that tricyclics are usually to be preferred in such patients.

V.   Other psychotropic agents

Psychotropic agents such as sedatives or phenothiazine-like preparations have not in our experience caused difficulties. We once limited the use of diazepam (Valium) and chlordiazepoxide (Librium) to smaller than usual doses but now start with the lower dose at times but build up to a full dose in most cases. We have not had problems with the addition of phenothiazines.

VI.   Alcohol

On occasion patients knowingly or unknowingly take alcohol. The response is quite unpredictable with a few showing extraordinary sensitivity and most tolerating ordinary portions without clinical symptoms. Certainly the prohibition should be continued although a substantial number of patients sooner or later confess that they are taking one or two drinks when they go to a party or even on a regular basis. If a patient cannot be prevented from using alcohol it seems wiser to continue the prohibition but indicate that hard liquor is probably safer than wine or quantities of beer.

VII.   Opiates

We have usually recommended that patients being given narcotics or anesthetics be tried on one quarter of the usual dose if they could not previously be removed from medication for a week in advance. This applied to meperidine (Demerol). In view of reported results probably other narcotics would be preferable. There have been no problems in respect to patients having dental work done as a result of the cocaine-related derivatives. There has sometimes been increased jitteriness as a result of the epinephrine usually present in such injections. In most cases we have suggested that the dentist use so called 'cardiac' Novocaine, Xylocaine, etc. to largely eliminate the parenteral epinephrine.

VIII.   Meperidine (Demerol)

This has been previously discussed (E-2-d-VII)

IX.   Cocaine, Procaine and related preparations

This has been previously discussed (E-2-d-VII)

X.   Antihypertensive agents

Our experience with the addition of diuretic antihypertensive agents has not provoked any problems. Reserpine is discussed elsewhere.

XI.   Parenteral guanethidine

Lack of experience with this preparation makes comment impossible.

XII.   Anesthetics (especially ether)

Based on the experience of patients on MAOIs receiving emergency operations we have not been impressed that inhalation anesthesia carries any great danger. As a matter of caution we recommend removal of patients from MAOIs one to two weeks prior to elective procedures and suggest closer than usual supervision during anesthesia.

Of much greater danger in conjunction with operative procedures is the use of scopolamine, atropine and similar anticholinergic agents especially if given in high doses and particularly if administered parenterally. Their action is dangerously potentiated.

XIII.   Foods and beverages (cheese)

It is apparently the presence of tyramine and possibly a few related chemicals that can cause a dramatic and sometimes fatal increase in blood pressure. The reaction to unprocessed, highly fermented cheese is well-known. Headaches following meals should lead one to suspect that the patient may be 'cheating' on prohibited foods. In extreme cases there have been cerebral hemorrhages which has led to the recommendation of avoiding MAOIs in patients with any suspicion of a cerebrovascular defect.

More detailed discussion of food restrictions is contained in the pamphlet 'So You Have A Depression' [17] which is included later in this paper.

XIV.   Foods and beverages (pickled herring)

This has been previously discussed (E-2-d-XIII)

XV.   Foods and beverages (Chianti, beer, yeast extract)

This has been previously discussed (E-2-d-XIII)

XVI.   Foods and beverages (chicken liver)

This has been previously discussed (E-2-d-XIII)

XVII. Foods and beverages (pods of broad beans)

This has been previously discussed (E-2-d-XIII)

XVIII. Foods and beverages (canned figs)

This has been previously discussed (E-2-d-XIII)

XIX. Reserpine and parenteral reserpine

Until there is more information probably the prohibition against reserpine (particularly parenteral reserpine) is a wise one. Interestingly HIMWICH [7] has recommended the addition of reserpine, either oral or parenteral, for patients on tricyclics who have not responded to the tricyclic alone. He has not recommended such use with MAO inhibitors.

XX. Antihistaminics

Except for the fact that in some patients smaller than usual doses are effective, the antihistaminics have not caused difficulties.

XXI. Diuretics

This has been previously discussed (E-2-d-X)

XXII. DOPA, dopamine, tryptophane

Contrary to the caution against combinations we have found as has COPPEN, SHAW, MALLESON, ECCLESTON and GUNDY [3] that tryptophane or its derivative 5-HTP has often improved the patient's condition when he was not otherwise responding [20–22]. There is good evidence that DOPA raises blood pressure and we have carried out some studies which show it to be of some usefulness in the treatment of orthostatic hypotension [5]. We lack experience with dopamine.

XXIII. Antiparkinsonian agents

We have not noticed any particular difficulty with antiparkinsonian agents except that at times they have a tendency to produce toxic psychoses (with or without MAOIs) and this is more frequent than is generally recognized. As long as anticholinergic action has not interfered with bowel function the drugs have given us no problem on this score.

XXIV. Over-the-counter preparations

Many over-the-counter preparations in addition to the ones already mentioned contain substances (atropine, caffeine, etc.) which are known to be at least mildly incompatible with MAOIs and possibly dangerous in high doses. Other such products contain substances whose reactions with MAOIs are unknown. As far as possible their use should be avoided or if for some reason they are permitted the amount per dose should be markedly reduced until the effects on a particular patient are known.

XXV. Sympathomimetics

Amphetamines and some of the other sympathomimetics have been discussed above. In most cases other members of this class may be used but initial dosage should be about $\frac{1}{4}$ to $\frac{1}{2}$ of the usual until effects are known.

XXVI. Parenteral reserpine

This has been previously discussed (E-2-d-XIX)

XXVII. Caffeine

In markedly sensitive individuals even a small amount of caffeine may be potentiated so as to produce jitteriness. In most patients the amount of caffeine in 3 or 4 cups of tea or coffee per day does not lead to any reactions. Extremely large amounts of caffeine do appear to be potentiated in other patients.

e)   *Addendum*

As previously indicated, if a relationship can be shown between the time of ingestion of the MAO inhibitor and the response to foods containing tyramine or alcohol then almost all the above recommendations could possibly be modified.

F.   Side Effects and Their Management

1.   Tricyclics

a)   *Side effects as seen in clinical usage*

The most persistent and annoying side effect from the tricyclics is dryness of the mouth. Some patients disregard the side effect, most tolerate it more or less unwillingly and a few refuse to continue medication.

Another of the anticholinergic actions of the drug, constipation, is almost as common. This is more of a problem than usual since most such patients already have the beginning of somatic concerns.

The third of the important and almost inevitable side effects is difficulty in focusing because of weakness of the muscles of accomodation.

Other problems which arise are unusual enough that they need not necessarily be discussed with the patient in advance.

b)   *FDA package insert derived list of tricyclic side effects*

These are listed in table VII.

c)   *Criticism of FDA derived listing of side effects*

Certainly weakness and related symptoms occur with imipramine as frequently as with the other tricyclics and euphoria also occurs at times with nortriptyline. The same would appear to be true of almost all the other

Table VII. Side effects of tricyclics as derived from FDA approved package inserts (as of 1967)

	amitriptyline (Elavil)	desipramine (Norpramin, Pertofrane)	imipramine (Tofranil)	nortriptyline (Aventyl)
Orthostatic hypotension	+	+	+	+
Dizziness, vertigo, fainting, tachycardia (without hypotension)	+	+	+	+
Weakness, fatigue, lethargy, drowsiness	+	+		+
Constipation	+	+	+	+
Dryness of mouth	+	+	+	+
Gastro-intestinal disturbance	+	+	+	+
Jaundice and liver damage	+	+	+	
Overactivity, overstimulation, jitteriness, agitation	+	+	+	+
Euphoria, hypomania, mania	+	+	+	
Hyperreflexia, tremors, muscle twitching, nystagmus, akathisia, extrapyramidal symptoms	+	+	+	+
Paresthesias, tinnitus, arthralgia, neuritis	+	+	+	+
Memory impairment, palilalia, ataxia, confusion, incontinence, toxic delirium, hallucinations, coma	+	+	+	+
Seizures	+	+	+	+
Headache	+	+		+
Blurred vision (accommodation difficulty)	+	+	+	+
Hematologic changes	+	+		
Edema (peripheral, glottal, orbital)				+
Body weight change (usually increase)	+			+
Appetite change (usually increase)	+			+
Skin sensitivity (rash, flushing, photo-sensitivity, telangiectasis)	+	+	+	+
Hyperhidrosis (sweating)	+	+	+	+
Dysuria (micturition difficulty, retention, frequency)	+	+	+	+
Sexual disturbances (impotence, delayed ejaculation)			+	+
Insomnia			+	+
Nightmares				+
Bone marrow depression			+	+

omissions on table VII so that in general it can be stated that if a side effect appears with one tricyclic it in all probability occurs with the other tricyclics.

The second problem with the present listing is that it provides no idea of frequency of occurrence. It is to be hoped that eventually some system will be created which will remedy this deficiency. There are difficulties and confusions which arise because of the present method of deriving such lists of side effects. It is required that any aberrant or pathological finding which occurs while a patient is receiving medication be reported to the FDA and/or the pharmaceutical company. As a rule once a purported side effect has been reported (even erroneously) it is likely to be perpetuated indefinitely.

d)   Management of side effects

I.   Orthostatic hypotension

A drop of 10% in both systolic and diastolic pressure is not unusual in the first few weeks of treatment. This is subject to homeostatic adjustment and as a rule returns to normal within a month. Even when the drop is more marked no treatment is indicated unless the patient complains of symptoms.

In many cases additional medication can be avoided if the patient learns how to handle himself. The hypotension usually is most manifest when the patient arises during the night to go to the toilet or in the morning when he or she goes to the bathroom. Arising abruptly and/or standing in one place may lead to sufficient drop in blood pressure to produce syncope and the patient may be hurt in falling. By getting out of bed slowly and by shifting weight from one foot to the other while standing, the syncope can often be avoided. The same applies to daytime activity and for women the addition of a girdle and supportive hosiery are helpful. If medications are needed anti-hypotensive drugs such as mephentermine sulfate (Wyamine) in doses of 12–½ to 25 mg 3 to 5 times a day or ephedrine sulfate in doses of 1/16 to 1/8 grain 4 to 5 times a day will often bring the blood pressure up to normal. In more persistent cases fludrocortisone (Florinef) in doses ranging from 0.1 to 1.0 mg a day will often be successful where other measures have failed.

As previously stressed even though the blood pressure is persistently below 100 and sometimes as low as 80/60 there is still no indication for medication or other treatment unless symptoms occur.

II.   Dizziness, vertigo, fainting, tachycardia (without hypotension)

These symptoms if they occur tend to do so early in the course of treatment. The most useful way of handling the problem is to reduce the dosage by half and administer all medication at bedtime. As a rule within one week sufficient adjustment occurs so that symptoms disappear. If not sufficient a small dose of a sedative may be of some help. If there has been no relief within a week it is suggested that an alternate medication be substituted.

III.   Weakness, fatigue, lethargy, drowsiness

Patients should be forewarned of the likelihood that such reactions will occur during the first week of being placed on medication. If the symptoms persist beyond a few days the addition of one of the psychomotor stimulants in ordinary doses will usually provide relief. As a rule the symptoms disappear within a week or ten days and then the psychomotor stimulant should be gradually decreased. If these measures are not sufficient and the side effect is sufficiently severe it is recommended that after two to three weeks an alternate medication be substituted. Once again giving all the medication at bedtime is useful because the side effect thus sometimes becomes of therapeutic value. Occasionally psychomotor stimulants can also be administered under these circumstances.

IV.   Constipation

The occurrence of some degree of constipation is almost universal and, although in the majority of cases, after a number of weeks or months bowel habits return to within normal limits this is not always the case. Many patients are in the habit of producing one to two bowel movements a day and it is wise to caution them in advance that this frequency is likely to be reduced without loss of health to as little as one to two bowel movements a week. The use of preparations which increase bulk of bowel movements are occasionally useful as is mineral oil. If the patient in the past has found these techniques useful or the addition of certain foods to the diet (such as prunes) he should be encouraged to use these methods. The next step would be the addition of a stool softening agent such as dioctyl sodium sulfosuccinate (Colace) given 100 mg two or three times a day. If this proves inadequate the addition of one of the saline cathartics such as milk of magnesia or citrate of magnesia every three or four days is in order. If absolutely essential one of the more ordinary peristaltic agents may be given occasionally but regular use usually leaves the gut in such condition that eventually a bowel movement without them is impossible. The possibility of enemas once or twice a week should not be overlooked as an alternative to some of the above.

V.   Dryness of the mouth

Dryness of the mouth is almost a universal complaint although sometimes this only comes to notice when the patient complains that his food seems to taste peculiar as a result of lessened supply of saliva. Over long periods of time there is usually some return of normal salivary flow but this is not always the case. Unless the patient finds the side effect most discomforting he should be encouraged to accept it as a minor handicap. In the past we have found, as have others, that pilocarpine is useful but unfortunately the improvement is usually only temporary. During the initial period of discomfort we have found that a glycerine based lozenge such as Pine Bros. cough drops frequently provides sufficient relief. Most of the other candies become cloyingly sweet after a short while.

VI.   Gastrointestinal disturbances

In our own experience when gastrointestinal disturbances occur they are usually of a temporary nature. If there is persistence beyond a week or ten days it would seem to indicate some idiosyncratic or allergic type reaction and substitution of an alternate preparation after two weeks would be in order if the patient is unable to tolerate the discomfort. This would include the occasional patient who develops diarrhea or loose stools rather than constipation.

VII.   Jaundice and liver damage

In our own experience the occurrence of such conditions has been extremely rare and always turned out to be a result of concurrent disorders rather than from the tricyclic. As a general caution we establish a baseline for laboratory work which includes four liver function tests which are usually repeated at the end of one month of medication and thereafter every three to six months. The occurrence of a minor increase above accepted norms in one of the four tests prior to medication is usually not regarded as a contraindication for starting treatment but the tests are then repeated more frequently. If an abnormality of test is found during the course of treatment it is recommended that the test be repeated before anything else is done. Should it be found that the abnormal index is still present it is recommended that the patient be referred to his or her family physician if facilities are not available for complete physical examination to determine if there is alternate cause other than drugs for the abnormality. If the deviation is grossly abnormal on more than one of the tests then it is probably wise to discontinue the tricyclic until the cause of the abnormality has been determined.

VIII.   Overactivity, overstimulation, jitteriness, agitation

Once these symptoms begin developing in the course of treatment it is unlikely that they will recede spontaneously with the patient on medication. If the patient is already showing improvement the recommended course would be to reduce the medication by half and allow a week for the side effect to disappear. If the extent of the side effect is marked a sedative can be added in ordinary dosages. This is especially the case when more prolonged treatment is indicated. Even somewhat preferable to this is to substitute a different member of the tricyclic group or to make use of one of the preparations which combines a tricyclic with a phenothiazine. Continued persistence would indicate the need for substitution of an MAO inhibitor since this side effect is usually less frequent with the MAOIs.

IX.   Euphoria, hypomania, mania

This side effect usually can easily be handled by reduction of the medication. In moderate to severe cases a phenothiazine should be added or a preparation combining the antidepressant and phenothiazine should be used together with reduction of dosage. In many cases the antidepressant medication can be totally discontinued but this is a matter of clinical judgment.

X.   Hyper-reflexia, tremors, muscle twitching, nystagmus, akathisia, extrapyramidal symptoms

The question of how to handle motor side effects has not been universally agreed upon. Antiparkinsonian agents in our experience have not been as satisfactory as reported. Sedatives are of assistance in some cases but our own preference has been for the addition of either diphenhydramine (Benadryl) or one of the milder phenothiazines such as promazine (Sparine).

XI.   Paresthesias, tinnitus, arthralgia, neuritis

In these cases we usually substitute one of the alternate preparations but at times the use of Vitamin B (50 mg b.i.d.) and Vitamin B$_{12}$ (100 mcg b.i.d.) provide relief after two to three weeks of usage. If the side effect is not severe we usually encourage the patient to accept the inconvenience.

XII.   Memory impairment, palilalia, ataxia, confusion, incontinence, toxic delirium, hallucinations, coma

Obviously the more severe degrees of this progression indicate immediate discontinuance of medication. If there is no problem of agitated behavior the recommendation is to discontinue all medication but if control is necessary substantial doses of phenothiazines may be indicated. Again we prefer to withhold medication or use only a mild sedative such as diphenhydramine (Benadryl), or promazine (Sparine) PRN. If the patient is still in need of treatment for depression it is often sufficient to withdraw medication for 24 to 48 hours and then to restore it at a lower dosage level. In some patients, particularly the older ones, an accumulation of toxic effects does appear to occur. We have not been advocates of a regular 'drug holiday' (e.g. 'Never on Sunday') for the ordinary patient. However, in those individuals who periodically do seem to develop toxic reactions we have used this procedure successfully. As a rule the patient can be returned to half dose and then full dose with instructions to the family that should a similar episode recur, once again the tricyclic medication should be discontinued for the 24 to 48 hours.

The question of how to handle a mild degree of memory impairment is most difficult since this is often a symptom of the depression itself. The patient usually first notices this condition after improvement of the depression and then attributes it to the medication. In addition most normal individuals have considerably poorer memories than is generally believed and hence when patients on medication begin paying attention to such functions they blame a natural state on the medication. If there is serious doubt and when the impairment is a great inconvenience it is sometimes worth first substituting an alternate medication and if this is unsuccessful to test the patient off of medication for two to three weeks to determine whether there is any improvement of memory. As a rule there is not, but the procedure at least serves to reassure both the patient and the physician that the memory loss is not the result of treatment.

XIII.   Seizures

The epileptic threshold is definitely reduced and an increase in anticonvulsant medication is often indicated. In some cases seizures are precipitated for the first time but if the medication is working effectively otherwise it is advisable to continue but to add suitable preparations to prevent recurrence of seizures.

XIV.   Headache

Headache is such a frequent occurrence in depressions that it is often difficult to determine whether this is due to medication. It can be controlled by ordinary analgesics if there is no contraindication for their use. In cases of persistence and if they are severe enough it is recommended that an alternate preparation be used or the patient changed to one of the MAO inhibitors.

XV.   Blurred vision

Distance vision is unimpaired but reading, sewing, or anything requiring near vision is apt to be distorted because of the accommodation difficulty. Here again it is wise to caution the patient of the possibility of such an occurrence so that he does not feel that in addition to everything else he is developing a brain tumor or losing his sight. Over the years we have tried a variety of medications and although some of them give temporary or partial relief the most practical solution is to wait until the patient has accumulated sufficient medication so that the effects are probably stable and then to have glasses made which help compensate for the lack of adequate accommodation. The old lens should be saved not only to be used again when the patient is off medication but because in a reasonable number of cases the body does a good job of compensating over the course of several months so that near vision is often returned to almost normal. Obviously when the drug is discontinued the impairment is removed.

XVI.   Hematologic changes

These have not occurred in our experience and the data in the literature are not sufficient to make an adequate statement.

XVII.   Edema

Various types of edema including peripheral, glottal and orbital have been reported. We were able to confirm the occurrence of this side effect but have not developed a completely satisfactory method of handling it. As a rule we have used diuretic agents but rather sparingly. The occurrence of the edema may well be due to an electrolyte imbalance following changes in membrane permeability. Study of electrolytes in these patients would appear to be in order and we hope to undertake such an investigation which hopefully could result in developing a technique of management.

XVIII. Body weight change

A substantial number of patients report a substantial gain of weight. In many cases the patients are insistent that this is without increase in food uptake. Whether such an increase is due totally to accumulation of fluids or whether there is actually some change in metabolic function has not been determined. This is another of the studies we are planning to undertake in the near future. Certainly in a large number of the cases the patient upon beginning to feel better also starts eating considerably more. This is not necessarily at mealtimes and hence the patients and their families often protest that there has been no increase in food intake whereas calories in the form of soft drinks, cake, and between-meal candy has actually increased considerably. As a rule we have not found the usual anorexients to be of much use but have sent these patients to the Weight Watchers or similar organizations with much better results. Since much of the overwhelming compulsion to eat occurs at night, one useful technique is to substitute an hypnotic to be taken before the usually fateful hour arrives.

XIX.   Appetite change

Formerly depressed patients who had poor appetites almost invariably show improvement in this respect which in turn often results in a body weight change. Should there be no improvement in appetite the physician should be suspicious of claims on the part of the patient that he is feeling much better since on occasion these patients present a real suicidal risk, i.e. those in whom there is improvement of affect without concomitant physiological improvement.

XX.   Skin sensitivity

The occurrence of perspiration and flushing is discussed in the next item under hyperhidrosis. There are occasional idiosyncratic rashes which appear to be on an allergic basis and which frequently can be managed successfully with antihistaminic medication if the patient is doing well otherwise. The occurrence of photo-sensitivity is quite rare and the one reported case in the literature would not seem to be sufficient in our opinion.

XXI.   Hyperhidrosis (sweating)

The appearance of 'heat waves', flushing and attacks of hyperhidrosis which occasionally are extremely marked is more common with the use of tricyclics than is generally recognized. Usually the episodes last from 3 to 20 minutes. We have found no satisfactory method of preventing their occurrence nor of managing them beyond reassuring the patient of the commonness of their occurrence and the fact that they are not indicative of any known danger or pathology.

XXII.   Dysuria

Delayed micturition is not infrequent and sometimes can result in urinary retention. This is especially true of patients with prostate difficulties or history or the presence of genito-urinary tract infections. The problem can be a quite persistent one and, if it is not satisfactorily removed by the treatment of the underlying physical condition, a change to the use of monamine oxidase inhibitors is recommended since urinary retention is less frequent with this group of drugs.

Urinary frequency appears related to a greater sensitivity to bladder pressure and may account for the usefulness of this group of drugs in the treatment of enuresis.

XXIII. Sexual disturbances

Impotence and delayed ejaculation occur occasionally but much less frequently than with the monamine oxidase inhibitors. As a rule the various changes which occur could be classified under the head of reduced sexual sensitivity. As a rule there is return of normal function although this may take a number of months. At times it is necessary to substitute an alternate preparation. In patients suffering from premature ejaculation the antidepressants become useful as a specific method of treatment even though depression is not present.

In a previous publication we have commented upon the increase in sperm count which sometimes follows the use of these drugs. There is also some evidence of increased fertility on the part of the female patients and hence there is the 'danger' that if either patient is placed upon an antidepressant drug one of the side effects may be pregnancy if the couple had reason to believe on the basis of past experience that they were no longer fertile and hence were not using any type of contraception.

XXIV. Insomnia

There is often definitely reduced sleep need which is even more marked with the monamine oxidase inhibitors. There is no contraindication to the use of sleeping medications and hence if a patient was on these previously they can usually be continued although a somewhat lower dose should be given initially. It is important to explain to the patient that three-to-four hours a night's sleep is really all that appears to be requisite and as long as he is not fatigued or sleepy during the day he should not feel under any great requirement to insist upon eight hours a night of sleeping. For the occasional patient who shows drowsiness in the late afternoon it is remarkable how sometimes a half hour nap is sufficient to revive the patient without the use of additional medications.

It is advisable to warn the patient in advance that reduced sleep need may occur. It can be pointed out to him that this is a great advantage since if he feels somewhat better he will be able to do many of the things he was unable to do while depressed.

XXV. Nightmares

Certainly these are reported by some patients using tricyclics but how and in what way they are related to any of the antidepressant medications is unclear. Studies on the effects of these drugs on REM (Rapid Eye Movement) time are underway but the evidence is not conclusive one way or the other at present.

XXVI. Bone marrow depression

The report of bone marrow depression appears to be an isolated one and we have had no evidence that it constitutes a real danger or is even a real side effect.

2.   Monamine Oxidase Inhibitors

a)   Side effects as seen in clinical usage

A major side effect of the monamine oxidase inhibitors in ordinary clinical usage is orthostatic hypotension. Constipation is an almost universal occurrence and it must be emphasized to the patient that a bowel movement once or twice a week is perfectly adequate. Weight increase is also quite common and we have found persuading the patient to join an organization such as the Weight Watchers Club is more effective than the usual anorexiants. Reduced sleep need can be a problem if the patient insists upon getting eight hours a night sleep because in order to do this he will often have to oversedate himself. There is also not infrequently reduced sexual sensitivity about which the patient should be warned in advance since if he is still active sexually despite the depression the occurrence of impotence will only make him feel more depressed.

Table VIII. Side effects of MAO inhibitors as derived from FDA approved package inserts

	isocarboxazid (Marplan)	nialamide (Niamid)	phenelzine (Nardil)	tranylcypromine (Parnate)	pargyline (Eutonyl)
Orthostatic hypotension	+	+	+	+	+
Dizziness, vertigo, fainting, tachycardia (without hypotension)	+	+	+	+	+
Weakness, fatigue, lethargy, drowsiness	+	+	+	+	
Hypertension		+	+		
Constipation	+	+	+	+	+
Dryness of mouth	+	+	+	+	+
Gastro-intestinal disturbance	+	+	+	+	+
Jaundice and liver damage			+		
Chills and fever				+	+
Overactivity, overstimulation, jitteriness, agitation	+		+	+	+
Euphoria, hypomania, mania	+	+	+	+	
Hyperreflexia tremors, muscle twitching, nystagmus, akathisia, extrapyramidal symptoms	+		+		+
Paresthesias, tinnitus, arthralgia, neuritis	+			?	+
Memory impairment, palilalia, ataxia, confusion, incontinence, toxic delirium, hallucinations, coma	+		+		
Seizures		+	+	+	
Headache	+	+	+	+	+
Blurred vision (accommodation difficulty)	+	+	+	+	
Glaucoma			+		
Reduced blood sugar					+
Hypernatremia (excess sodium)			+		
Hematologic changes	+	+	+		
Edema (peripheral, glottal, orbital)	+		+	+	+
Body weight change (usually increase)	+				+
Appetite change (usually increase)	+			+	+
Skin sensitivity (rash, flushing, photo-sensitivity, telangiectasis)	+	+	+	+	+
Hyperhidrosis (sweating)	+	+	+		+
Dysuria (micturition difficulty, retention, frequency)	+		+	?	+
Sexual disturbances (impotence, delayed ejaculation)	+		+	+	
Insomnia					+
Nightmares					+

b)   *FDA package insert derived list of MAOI side effects*

The previous list (table VIII) includes the side effects itemized on the package inserts. In view of the fact that generally isocarboxyzid and nialamide are weak MAO inhibitors and phenelzine, tranylcypromine and pargyline are potent ones it is evident that there are some very marked inconsistencies in the list. Quite a number of the side effects listed are so rare as to be curiosities if they actually are drug-related at all.

c)   *Management of MAOI side effects*

I.   Orthostatic hypotension

It is not infrequent for patients to function perfectly adequately with blood pressure as low as 80/60 but with no clinical symptoms. It is more difficult for the physician to accept this than for the patient. Often the patient's physiology adjusts itself so that blood pressure returns to within normal limits and a medication should not be given unless the patient complains of symptoms. Initially we recommended antihypotensive agents to increase blood pressure whenever it fell below 100 systolic but often the patient would discontinue the drug spontaneously.

II.   Dizziness, vertigo, fainting, tachycardia (without hypotension)

The same recommendations apply as for the management of tri-cyclics.

III.   Weakness, fatigue, lethargy, drowsiness

The same recommendations apply as for the tricyclics.

IV.   Hypertension

Occurrence of hypertension usually indicates that the patient is on some food or medication which is being potentiated. If the increase in blood pressure is marked it is possible to reduce it quite rapidly by phentolamine (Regitine).

V.   Constipation

Recommendations are the same as for the tricyclics.

VI.   Dryness of the mouth

This condition is extremely rare with the MAOIs and when occurs glycerine based lozenges are to be preferred. Pilocarpine and similar preparations should be avoided.

VII.   Gastrointestinal disturbances

Recommendations are the same as for tricyclics.

VIII.   Jaundice and liver damage

Discontinuance of medication is in order until the cause of the jaundice has been determined.

IX.   Fever

Fever is probably the result of an allergic type of sensitivity if it does occur. Discontinuance of medication and retrial is in order if the fever was not excessive. If there is recurrence an alternate preparation should be used.

X.   Overactivity, overstimulation, jitteriness, agitation

Recommendations are the same as for tricyclics.

XI.   Euphoria, hypomania, mania

Recommendations are the same as for tricyclics. Incidentally the absence of such reported effects with pargyline does not indicate the absence of the manic effect but merely the absence of complete documentation in the list since we have seen a number of such cases of manic type response.

XII.   Hyperreflexia, tremors, muscle twitching, nystagmus, akathisia, extrapyramidal symptoms

Management is the same as for tricyclics.

XIII.   Paresthesias, tinnitus, arthralgia, neuritis

Recommendations are the same as for management of tricyclics.

XIV.   Memory impairment, palilalia, ataxia, confusion, incontinence, toxic delirium, hallucinations, coma

Recommendations are the same as for the tricyclics.

XV.   Seizures

Recommendations are the same as for tricyclics.

XVI.   Headache

Recommendations are the same as for tricyclics.

XVII.   Blurred vision

This in our experience is extremely rare on MAO inhibitors although it is listed as a side effect for each of the drugs except pargyline. Should it actually occur the recommendations would be the same as for management on tricyclics.

XVIII. Glaucoma

A single instance is reported. Obviously if there is some demonstrated connection (which now seems unlikely) medication should be discontinued.

XIX.   Reduced blood sugar

There is evidence that reduced blood sugar may occur on any of the MAO inhibitors and as indicated previously it is important insofar as it may be misleading if the patient is a diabetic or is suspected of hypoglycemia.

XX.   Hyponitremia

We have not seen evidence of sodium excess but if it does occur it might be the result of altered membrane permeability. As indicated previously more intense study of electrolytes in depression along the lines of the work by COPPEN is in order.

XXI.   Hematologic changes

We have had no experience of hematologic changes and hence cannot comment except that blood tests should be repeated before concluding that an actual change has occurred. It would probably be advisable to discontinue medication to see whether the condition disappeared. From the beginning other possible causes of hematological changes should be investigated.

XXII. Edema

Same recommendations are in order as under tricyclics.

XXIII. Body weight changes

Recommendations are the same as listed under tricyclics.

XXIV. Appetite change

Recommendations are the same as listed under tricyclics.

XXV. Skin sensitivity

See recommendations under tricyclics.

XXVI. Hyperhidrosis

See recommendations under tricyclics.

XXVII. Dysuria

See recommendations under tricyclics.

XXVIII. Sexual disturbances

See recommendations under tricyclics.

XXIX. Insomnia

See recommendations under tricyclics.

XXX. Nightmares

See recommendations under tricyclics.

G. Preparation of the Patient

1. How to Approach the Subject

The patient's past experience (or lack of it) will provide broad clues as to how the subject can best be approached. The psychiatrist is so often involved in the matter of explanations that he feels it mandatory to provide to the patient an explanation of why he is being given this particular preparation and how it is supposed to work. Very often this is not only unnecessary but a distinct hindrance. Obviously if the patient does seriously ask an explanation should be provided and in most cases the opportunity for asking should be made available by inquiring after instructions have been given 'Are there any questions you have?'. If there are no questions the matter should not be pursued.

It is an anomaly that a surprising number of patients are upset by the fact that their clinical condition improves but they 'don't understand' or 'haven't worked through' their reasons for recovery. This is undoubtedly related to the misunderstanding even and perhaps particularly by intelligent laymen that all psychiatric disorders have purely psychological causes and can be adequately treated only by 'insight' therapy. Usually the explanation that the problem can be approached physiologically as well and that the two types of treatment are not incompatible is sufficient.

2. Written Material

We have found it extremely reassuring to both the patient and his family to provide copies of the brochure 'So You Have a Depression!' which is modified somewhat from the original publication [17].

This material appears in the appendix.

References

1. BAASTRUP, P.C. and SCHOU, M.: Lithium as a prophylactic agent. Arch. gen. Psychiat. *16:* 162–172 (1967).
2. BARNETT, B.: Witchcraft, psychopathology and hallucinations. Brit. J. Psychiat. *111:* 439–445 (1965).
3. COPPEN, A.; SHAW, D.M.; MALLESON, A.; ECCLESTON, E. and GUNDY, G.: Tryptamine metabolism in depression. Brit. J. Psychiat. *111:* 993–998 (1965).
4. Evaluation of Drug-Treated Private Patients. Grant No. 1 R 10 MH 13446 Psychopharmacology Research Branch, National Institute of Mental Health.
5. FRIEND, D.G.; BELL, W.R. and KLINE, N.S.: The action of L-dihydroxyphenylalanine in patients receiving nialamide. Clin. Pharmacol. Ther. *6:* 362–366 (1965).
6. GERSHON, S. and YUWILER, A.: Lithium Ion: A specific psychopharmacological approach to the treatment of mania. J. Neuropsychiat. *1:* 229–241 (1960).
7. HIMWICH, H.: Personal Communication.
8. HORWITZ, W.A.: Physiological guides to antidepressant therapy. Excerpta med. Int. Congr. Series 122, pp. 353–359.
9. KLINE, N.S.: American Maudsley Bequest Lecture, London, England, May 14, 1965.
10. KLINE, N.S.: Correspondence with James L. Goddard, M.D., Commissioner of Food and Drugs. Amer. Coll. Neuropsychopharmacol. Bull. *5:* 1 (1967).
11. KLINE, N.S.: Drug treatment of phobic disorders. Amer. J. Psychiat. *123:* 1447–1450 (1967).
12. KLINE, N.S.: The dual action of drugs: Pharmaceutical and psychological. NeuroPsychopharmacology *4:* 263–265 (1965).
13. KLINE, N.S.: The practical management of depression. J. amer. med. Ass. *190:* 732–740 (1964).
14. KLINE, N.S.: The psychology, philosophy, morality and legislative control of drug usage. In: EFRON, D.H.; HOLMSTEDT, B. and KLINE, N.S. (eds.) Ethnopharmacologic Search for Psychoactive Drugs, p. XVII–XIX, Public Health Service Publication No. 1645, U.S. Government Printing Office, Washington, D.C. 1967.
15. KLINE, N.S.: A theoretic framework for transcultural psychiatry. Amer. J. Psychiat. *123:* 85–87 (1966).
16. KLINE, N.S.: The use of Lithium sulfate in 300 private ambulatory patients with affective disorders (in preparation).
17. KLINE, N.S. and LEHMANN, H.E.: Handbook of psychiatric treatment in medical pratice (Saunders, Philadelphia, Pennsylvania 1962).
18. KLINE, N.S.; SABA, M. and SOLHIZADEH, S.: The successful treatment of narcotic addiction with antidepressants (Presented at CINP meeting, Washington, D.C., March 1966). Excerpta Medica, Amsterdam, 1967.

19.   KLINE, N.S.; SABA, M.; SOLHIZADEH, S. and ALLAPOUR, S.: Narcotic addiction treated with mutabon. IV World Congress of Psychiatry, Excerpta Medica, International congress Series No. 117, 1966.

20.   KLINE, N.S. and SACKS, W.: Relief of depression within one day using an M.A.O. inhibitor and intravenous 5-HTP. Amer. J. Psychiat. *120:* 274–275 (1963).

21.   KLINE, N.S.; SACKS, W. and SIMPSON, G.M.: Further studies on: one day treatment of depression with 5-HTP. Amer. J. Psychiat. *121:* 379–381 (1964).

22.   KLINE, N.S.; SIMPSON, G. and SACKS, W.: Amines and amine precursors combined with a monamine oxidase inhibitor in the treatment of depression. Proceedings of the Collegium Internationale Neuropsychopharmacologium Excerpta Medica, Amsterdam 1967.

23.   KLINE, N.S. and SWENSON, J.: Protriptyline (Vivactil) response relative to diagnosis in 80 depressed patients (in preparation).

24.   SNEZHNEVSKY, A.V.: Personal communication, 1965.

25.   WASSON, R.G.: Fly agaric and man. In: EFRON, D.H.; HOLMSEDT, B. and KLINE, N.S. (eds.) Ethnopharmacologic Search for Psychoactive Drugs, pp. 405–414, Public Health Service Publication No. 1645, U.S. Government Printing Office, Washington, D.C., 1967.

26.   COLE, J.O. and WITTENBORN, J.R.: Editors, pharmacotherapy of depression (Thomas, Springfield, Ill. 1966).

Appendix: So You Have a Depression!

Instructions to patients on antidepressant drugs

Depression, which was once thought to be merely an unfortunate state of mind for which the depressed person was largely responsible himself, is now recognized as a very common and painful disease—for which, fortunately, highly successful types of medical treatment have become available. Depression seems to have had many victims throughout history, in all types of societies. In the United States today, millions of people are known to suffer from it.

What are the Symptoms of Depression?

If you have a depression, you almost surely have feelings of *pessimism, hopelessness and sadness*. To use a popular word, you feel 'blue' most or all of the time. Some patients are merely vaguely aware that they do not seem to be getting as much fun out of life as other people. Others are so thoroughly depressed that they describe themselves as feeling like weeping if anyone so much as looks at them.

Perhaps these feelings are particularly disturbing because you can see no reason for them; everything is going smoothly in your life, yet you still feel depressed. On the other hand, you may think that the circumstances of your life are making you sad—while your family and friends insist that your situation is not really that bad or that you are mistaken in thinking you are unfortunate.

There are several symptoms of depression besides these feelings of pessimism and sadness, and some of the symptoms do not even resemble what is popularly thought of as being blue or depressed. For example

Poor Concentration: You may have difficulty in concentrating. Perhaps you often read a newspaper or listen to a television program only to find you have not been able to retain anything of what you read, saw or heard.

Fatigue: You are quite likely to get tired very easily and lack the drive to get things done the way you used to.

Insomnia: You may want to sleep a great deal—but at the same time, when you go to bed you may not be able to get to sleep. It is even more common to awaken very early feeling exhausted, frightened and depressed.

Remorse: It is not unusual to feel guilty about things in the past that you think you should have done and did not do—or the opposite, to feel guilty about things you did do and feel you should not have done.

Guilt: Because of your illness there are many things you cannot do which would ordinarily be easy for you. This inability to function as well as you feel you should is apt to produce feelings of guilt. You may feel that you are being unfair to your family.

Indecision: One of the most common symptoms is an inability to decide about things, even the most simple matters at times.

Concern: People in depressions are concerned about using up their resources. Often they will find it difficult to spend money even when they know the amount involved is unimportant.

Reduced Sexual Activity: Interest in sex and sexual performance usually declines to a remarkably low level for the depressed patient.

Decreased Love and Affection: You may feel shocked to discover that you feel little or no love any more for those persons among your friends and family who have always been extremely close to you in the past.

General Loss of Interest: You may well find yourself indifferent to all sorts of people, things and ideas that were once of great importance to you.

Anxiety: Besides being depressed, you may be tense, anxious or frightened. These feelings are so strong in some patients that they cover up the underlying depression.

Irritability: All sorts of trivial things may irritate you and you may not be able to control your annoyance and impatience.

Suicidal Thoughts: Almost everyone thinks of committing suicide at one time or another, but naturally such ideas are more frequent during a depression. Often this seems the only escape from an intolerable situation. These ideas will disappear when you start to feel better. If you have such thoughts you should mention them to the doctor.

Unusual Thoughts and Urges: Frequently there is fear of someone near and dear to you dying. Oddly enough there are also times when depressed patients have the urge to harm those near and dear to them. This too is a symptom which should be brought to your doctor's attention.

Physical Changes: Constipation is not unusual; neither is dryness of the mouth. Loss of appetite is common and sometimes results in marked loss of weight. Curiously, some patients overeat. Many patients find themselves plagued by all sorts of aches and pains, some of which may be new and some of which may have been present before but were seldom noticed. Other physical reactions that may accompany depression include nausea, chest pains, stomach cramps, rapid breathing, sweating, coldness, numbness or tingling of the hands and feet—and particularly headaches or other odd feelings of pressure in the head, ears or neck.

Concern about Dying: Because of the physical symptoms (or even without them) you may feel that a terrible and untreatable disease process is destroying some part of your body or brain. You may believe that doctors fail to recognize it or will not tell you the truth about it.

What about these symptoms? All of this is part of a depression much as fever, diarrhea or inflammation may be part of some other illness. You need not have all the symptoms listed here (or you may have different ones), but at least some of them are common to all depressions.

When did Your Depression Begin?

It may have begun long ago. Physicians today treat many patients in their fifties, sixties or seventies who seem to have been depressed more or less continuously for their entire lives, ever since they were children. On the other hand, some people acquire depression for the first time at some particular period in their lives. It may begin gradually or suddenly. It may go away and return, or once it has occurred, it may continue without any relief. Some people swing back and forth between periods of depression, periods of normal feelings and periods when they feel so elated that they know that this 'high' in their mood cannot last.

How Long is Depression Likely to Last?

This depends on whether the depression is treated or not. Without treatment, the depression may go away by itself after a time or may last forever. With treatment, it is almost certain that the depression can be relieved within a reasonable period. Through experience, physicians have learned to predict quite accurately what is likely to happen. They usually can determine the nature of the depression, decide whether and how it should be treated, and forecast what will happen as a result of treatment after they have seen the patient a few times.

What is the Cause of Depression?

Unfortunately the answer is not clear cut. There are many theories about the causes of depression. Some theories are biochemical; some are psychological, and some combine both ideas. In other words, there are physicians who believe that depressions are the result of abnormal chemical processes in the brain and body. Others believe that unfortunate events in human relationships produce psychological defects that result in depression. And there are those who combine the ideas of biochemical and psychological defects.

It is sad but true that all of these hypotheses remain at the moment scientifically unproved. But we do know, fortunately, that as a practical matter, various depressions can be controlled by medication and the theoretical problem of cause and effect does not affect the treatment.

What Sorts of Treatment are There for Depressions?

Most depressions can now be treated adequately with a variety of medications. A decade ago this was not true but in the intervening years chemists, pharmacologists and physicians have developed a large number of compounds that successfully control the symptoms of depression. In rare cases electroshock treatment may be useful and for other patients psychoanalysis, but medications are usually quite sufficient.

Is Intensive Psychotherapy Necessary?

Many patients ask this question. The answer is that in most cases the medications alone are sufficient to relieve a depression and it is not necessary to enter formal psychotherapy, which is the treatment of emotional problems through discussion and understanding. In a few cases the physician may recommend deep psychotherapy for the relief of certain emotional disturbances that complicate the depression or that are causing other kinds of difficulties. Even in these cases, however, the physician ordinarily will suggest that the psychotherapy be delayed until medication has relieved the acute symptoms of depression, which usually make psychotherapy difficult and unproductive. A patient who is already receiving psychotherapy, of course, may be urged to continue.

What is the Probability That the Medication Will Work for You?

A most agonizing symptom, when it occurs, is the belief that the depression will go on forever. Yet, although every depressed person worries that he or she is 'the one on whom the medication won't work', the probability of your having a favorable response is extremely high. The doctor has several different types of medication; even if one is not successful, it is almost certain that another one will work. Incidentally, you cannot fight the medication. It will work whether you 'believe in it' or not.

How Long Will it Take for the Medication to Work?

In extremely rare cases patients report improvement within a matter of a few hours; at the other extreme there are instances in which it takes as long as 3 or 4 months. The average time before there is any evidence of change is between 3 and 4 weeks. Only a few signs of improvement are usually noticed at first. You will probably show those signs of improvement by paying more attention to what is going on around you. Next you will do some of the things that you have not done when you were the most depressed. As a rule the last thing that happens is for the patient to feel well.

Because there are many different kinds of depression and many different medications the physician may try first one drug then another. The first drug may actually make you feel worse, or it may produce somewhat unpleasant effects. The important thing to do is to report those unpleasant effects to your doctor and let him decide about what to do next. Sometimes that effect, unpleasant as it may be for you at the moment, is what he is looking for.

The whole process might be described as resembling a football game in which one side—the physician—changes his tactics depending upon the reaction of the other side—the depression. Thus, the doctor may change the type of medication, the size of each dose or the number of pills you should take, depending upon your reaction to the specific medical tactics he had used.

When you do first feel well again, you may do so only for a matter of minutes or hours, then the depression may return, and it may be another several days or even weeks before you again feel well. There may be half a dozen such up and down episodes before the symptoms are gone for good.

How Long Will Medication be Needed?

This cannot be answered in advance. After the symptoms have disappeared for a substantial length of time the physician will usually reduce the dosage by steps. Just as it took days or weeks for the medicine to work, it also takes days or weeks for it to stop working. If you skip one or two doses and find no change, *that proves nothing* since you are still 'being carried' on the medicine you took days or weeks before.

The dose must be reduced slowly to determine what effect lessened amounts have. It is possible you may be able to go entirely without the medication, but in other cases small 'maintenance doses' may be desirable for the time being. A new and different medication may be given to prevent another depression from occurring. At the very worst, that would mean taking a few pills a day for a long period—as is done by hundreds of thousands of people who have insufficient vitamins, thyroid deficiency, diabetes, heart conditions, etc.

From time to time the doctor will check up on you to determine if you still need treatment and to see that you do not have any serious effects from taking the medication over a long term.

Will the Depression Recur?

This is always a possibility, just as it is possible that a person who never had a depression before may get one for the first time. In some ways you are better off than the person who has never had a depression before—for you will know what it is and also will know that it will respond to treatment.

If the depressions recur in cycles, low doses of medication are sometimes used to prevent their return. In any case, since your physician has already taken you through the period of determining which medication does work, you have 'money in the bank' because he knows which drug is likely to act most rapidly and effectively in your case.

What Part Should the Family Play?

A person in a depression seriously doubts that recovery is possible and he feels it will go on forever. The family should understand that the probability of improvement is excellent and should give the patient every encouragement that he will get well.

Simple statements like 'everything is going to be all right' or 'you are going to be all right very soon' help the patient get over the unpleasant early period of depression. Most people do not *like* being depressed and will start acting, thinking and feeling normal as soon as they can.

Many families misunderstand. It is important for them to know that the patient cannot help being depressed. There is nothing a depressed individual can do to 'pull himself together' or to 'be grateful for what he has'. These remarks imply that he is being ill because he wants to be. Such comments can only deepen the patient's sense of guilt and depression, which probably is already too strong. The family that is unusually irritable or tries to 'provoke' or force the patient to respond only makes the patient worse and the situation more unpleasant.

How Much Medication?

It is silly and sometimes dangerous to take more or less of a drug than is prescribed. During a surgical operation neither the patient nor his family would think of telling the surgeon to 'cut a little deeper' or 'take out more on the left side'. It is equally ridiculous for the patient to add to or subtract from his medications on the basis of his own opinions. You go to a doctor for treatment because of his superior skill and knowledge. Follow his instructions.

At times the drugs are given in specific combinations and taking one without the other may produce unpleasant or even dangerous results. Twice as much medication will not bring about improvement more quickly and may actually slow down recovery as well as endanger life. Taking less medication than recommended or reducing the dose by yourself is not helping matters since this may prevent full recovery and lead to an early return of symptoms.

Which Medication?

Do not take medications other than those prescribed. Often a drug, even one which you have taken safely in the past, will act differently in combination with certain other medications. For this reason it is important to check with your physician whether additional medication is compatible with what you are already taking. Above all, do not accept medication from friends whose good intentions may result in sad effects. It is not unusual for a person to be going to more than one physician, but make certain that each one knows what the other is doing by having one get in touch with the other.

Listed below are ordinary over-the-counter medications which it is safe to use in average doses unless otherwise indicated.

Antibiotics	Mineral Oil
Aspirin	Citrate of milk of magnesia
Bufferin	Vitamins

Some of the chemicals that can be purchased over the counter or are found in food may interfere with treatment. Their use should be either entirely discontinued, strictly limited or used in great moderation as checked below unless the doctor gives clearance.

Alcohol (whether as beer, wine or whiskey)	Most nose sprays and 'anti-cold tablets'
APC, Empirin, Anacin or drugs containing caffeine	Laxatives
Coffee, tea or caffeine—containing soft drinks such as the 'colas' (more than 3 times a day)	Preparations to increase alertness or keep you awake
Most pills used to 'help you reduce'	Anti-motion-sickness drugs
	Antihistamines
	Thyroid extract and other hormones
	Barbiturates and other sleeping pills

A Special Caution

If an operation is needed, be absolutely certain that the surgeon knows you are on an antidepressant medication. Injections of amphetamines, adrenalin, scopolamine, atropine and similar substances may be dangerous when given with certain antidepressants but not with others. Even morphine, codeine and Demerol must be used cautiously. A local anesthetic for dental work is permissible if the amount of adrenalin is low. Always ask if you are in doubt.

Do the Medications Have Side Effects?

In addition to their benefits, *most* drugs have additional minor actions. These are called side reactions and are usually not detrimental to your health. There is no major drug with a major effect on any disease process that is free of such side effects. In fact, research scientists are often suspicious of chemicals that have no side effects because they are also not likely to have major beneficial effects.

Before any pharmaceutical is placed on the market, however, it is tested extensively to be as certain as possible that the side effects are not dangerous. Even if there were a risk to the medication it is well to remember that the benefits to be gained from the drugs far outweigh any possible danger or minor inconvenience. As you read through the side effects below, keep in mind that any of them (or even all of them) do not compare at all in severity or danger with the depression itself.

Nevertheless it is important to report such symptoms when you see your doctor. The report will help him to chart the course of your treatment and also to eliminate the side effects if it becomes too unpleasant.

Reactions of this type vary greatly from one patient to another and at times a particular medication will produce an unpleasant side effect in one patient whereas another medication which is almost but not quite identical will have no unpleasant effect.

Although there are many side effects from the various medications, these are the most common ones:

'Peculiar' feelings: You are taking a medication designed to change your feelings. You should not be surprised, therefore, if you have a somewhat strange sensation. Usually this represents a period of adjustment which lasts only three or four days. If the feeling lasts longer, you should report it to your physician.

Change in Bowel Movements: Some of the medications will reduce the number of bowel movements. This is not necessarily constipation and usually not cause for alarm. Some people have the idea that there is something wrong if they do not have a bowel movement every day. Actually, the body can adjust equally well to having bowel movements only every three or four days. If you do experience a reduced number in bowel movements while you are taking medication for your depression, there is usually no need for laxatives or cathartics. A mild constipation frequently adjusts itself over a period of a few weeks.

No medication other than mineral oil should be taken without your doctor's advice. Most of the common treatments for constipation are safe but check with your doctor first.

Sleep Changes: A reduced need for sleep occurs as treatment progresses. This will be particularly noticeable for those patients whose main symptom has been an inordinate desire to sleep and who have spent long hours in bed. Many patients find after a time they can get along quite well on three or four hours of sleep a night. There is no proof that the body needs more than this to function healthily and efficiently.

If there is a reduction in the amount of sleep or if you have trouble getting to sleep, it is of course important to let your physician know it. *But do not take sleeping medication without your doctor's specific knowledge and approval.* Certain sleeping medications can prove dangerous in combination with the drugs used for depression if they are not specifically and properly prescribed.

Even if you have used a particular sleeping pill in the past without difficulty, this may no longer be true since the medications you are taking may make the sleeping pills act in a different way or to quite a different degree.

If you find that you are remaining awake two or three or four extra hours a night, be grateful; as you feel better you will have time to do many things that you could not do in the past because you were too depressed. When the medicine is decreased or discontinued your sleeping will return to its normal pattern.

Physical reactions: Sometimes you will experience minor but annoying reactions such as an increased amount of sweating, also dryness of the mouth. If the dryness of the mouth is too annoying the use of a glycerine-based cough drop (like Pine Brothers) will help relieve that particular symptom. At times blood pressure decreases which may produce some feelings of dizziness or weakness. Usually the body rapidly adjusts, but if not, there are medications to correct this side effect so that you can continue on antidepressant treatment.

Menstruation: Irregular or delayed menstruation is common and is no cause for concern. You should report it to your doctor, however, just as you should report any other changes.

Sex Drive: Some patients experience a temporary reduction in their sex drive. When the medication is reduced or discontinued there is complete recovery. In some cases changing to a different type of antidepressant will solve the problem. But you must tell your doctor about it or else he will not be able to help you. In any case, this also is not a cause for alarm.

In some patients in whom the depression has already reduced sexual activity, the medication may have a stimulant effect.

Blurred Vision: At times blurred vision, especially when reading, results soon after starting medication. It usually disappears fairly soon but if not can be corrected by reading glasses. After you go off medication this side effect disappears.

Questions?

Your doctor is there to help you. If you find you are forgetting to ask things you think important you might mail the list in advance so that questions can be answered completely and quickly when you arrive at the doctor's office. Sometimes it is a good idea to make a little list for yourself so that you can bring the queries along when you visit the physician.

One Last Word!

The most important single fact about depression is that it can be controlled by medication. This achievement is relatively new—so your friends and relatives may express disheartening or disbelieving thoughts about the possibilities of treatment. During the early period while the physician is trying to find the right medication you yourself may become discouraged. This is a common reaction. The way to handle it is to talk to your physician and not to allow the opinion of anyone else to influence you. Remember that your physician has many different drugs available to treat your case—at least one of which will almost surely work.

Is There Anything Else You can do?

Yes! When you are relieved you can reassure others that depression is a disease and not a weakness or punishment.

Much medical research is supported by Federal, State or local government. You can indicate by letter and by vote that you favor continuing and expanding these activities.

Finally, you can contribute to non-profit private organizations and foundations which provide psychiatric services, educate the public and underwrite the cost of psychiatric research.

Lithium:
The History of its Use in Psychiatry

When the full story of lithium is known it may contain a number of surprises. Although no reference to lithium as such appears in ancient Greek, Roman or Arabic sources there is a very good reason for this: the first identification was not made until 1817. A. ARFVEDSON found that the sodium compounds separated out from the mineral petalite were contaminated by another alkali which did not respond to the chemical tests for potassium, the only other alkali known at that time. His professor, the great Swedish physician-chemist, Baron JÖNS JAKOB BERZELIUS, named this oxide *lithion* (later changed to *lithia*) because it was found in rocks. Although small amounts of the free metal may have been produced by Sir HUMPHRY DAVY, it was first isolated in quantity by R. BUNSEN and A. MATTHIESSEN who electrolyzed the fused chloride in 1855.

General recognition of lithium's unique and remarkable characteristics came too late for it to be included in theories of alchemy and astrology. What a joy Paracelsus would have had with a substance which among other properties is

a) the lightest of all solid elements

b) but is the hardest of the alkali metals

c) next to water, the substance with the highest specific heat

d) when combined to form lithium fluoride, one of the most stable compounds known and

e) very strongly attractive to water molecules and in the reaction liberates exceptional amounts of energy.

As quantities of material became available it was immediately and mistakenly used in medicine [LIPOWITZ, 1841; GARROD, 1859] for the treatment of uremia, renal calculi, gout, rheumatism and allied disorders because in the test tube lithium carbonate combined with uric acid in a soluble form and even dissolved the urate deposits on cartilage. Since they became soluble these undesired substances could then be excreted in the urine—theoretically. Unfortunately the presence of sodium and potassium in the blood altered the reaction so that the amount of lithium required to form diuretic lithium urate far exceeded therapeutic limits.

Based on this simplistic observation the use of lithium salts did however extend far beyond medical prescription. Almost all the bottled 'curative' waters now on the market (Vichy, Appolonaire, Perrier, etc.) were at one time advertised for their high lithium content.

In 1927 CULBRETH noted that lithium was the most hypnotic of bromides and a bit later SQUIRES claimed it to be the most effective against epilepsy.

The next major but brief excursion of lithium into medicine occurred in 1949 when lithium chloride was proposed as a flavor and seasoning substitute for sodium chloride in those patients in whom salt intake was to be restricted. Again the fates were most unkind since the two major contraindications to lithium are now known to be cardiac and renal decompensation. These, of course, were precisely the patients to whom much of the lithium chloride was given with disastrous consequences. The resultant deaths from accumulation of toxic doses of lithium unquestionably retarded the broader usage of lithium in psychiatric treatment by at least a decade.

Yet the use of alkaline waters for the treatment of mania (including depression) has an old and honorable tradition. It is from CAELIUS AURELIANUS, a 5th century African physician from Numidia, that we have most of our knowledge of the wisdom of SORANUS (born in Greece, trained in Alexandria, practiced in Rome) who ranks with GALEN as one of the great physicians of the ancient world. In his section on the treatment of mania he writes:

> utendum quoque naturalibus aquis, ut sunt nitrosae
> Use should also be made of natural waters, such as alkaline springs.

The tradition of natural spring water for the treatment of emotional disturbances persisted so that in the current issue of HENDERSON and GILLESPIE's 'Textbook of Psychiatry' there appears:

CAELIUS 'modestly' begins the Preface to his works with:
'Aiunt Ippallum pythagoricum philosophum interrogatum quid ageret, respondisse "nondum nihil: nondum quidem mihi invidetur." si igitur proficientium testis est invidia, quae nobis olim comes est, magna gerimus in his quae gerimus.

It is said that the Pythagorean philosopher Hippasus, when asked what he had accomplished, replied: "Nothing as yet; at any rate, I am not yet an object of envy." If, then, envy is evidence of accomplishment, my achievements in my own field may be considered noteworthy, since they have long been an object of envy.

In medieval Europe certain wells were considered to have special virtue. Of these the most famous were St. Fillans, St. Ronans, Struthill, and a well on a small island on Loch Maree in Scotland; St. Winifred's Well in Wales; and some in England particularly in Cornwall. The valley of Glen-Na-Galt in Ireland had more than a local reputation.'

How interesting it would be to know the lithium content of these waters. Perhaps some British reader can enlighten us on this score!

The first deliberate use of lithium for the treatment of disturbed patients resulted from the experiments of an Australian psychiatrist, CADE, who was evaluating whether uric acid enhanced the toxicity of urea injected intraperitoneally into guinea pigs. Because of the insolubility of uric acid in water he used its most soluble salt—lithium urate—which did provide some protection against the convulsive deaths produced by toxic doses of urea. To determine whether lithium salts *per se* had any effect he gave an 0.5% aqueous solution of lithium carbonate to guinea pigs and found that two hours after injection, although fully conscious, the experimental animals were lethargic and unresponsive to stimuli. CADE'S overall objective was to determine if there were some excreted toxic substance in the urine of manic patients. He was a good enough clinician to have it occur to him that if the lithium calmed the guinea pigs it might very well do the same for manic patients so that, in his own words, 'the association of ideas is explicable'.

All 10 of the acute male manic patients he initially tested showed improvement; excitement in 6 cases of dementia praecox was lessened but 3 depressed patients showed no change.

One year later the next report to appear was of a death resulting from lithium used for psychiatric purposes, followed shortly by a letter to the editor describing successful use in more than 50 patients without fatalities and a year after that by the first formal confirmatory paper. In the interim the French, beginning with Despinoy, started using lithium for all types of excitement states (including manic ones). The first 5 years (see tables I and VI) concluded on a sour note with an article by an Italian, GIUSTINO, which is one of the very few papers in the literature not reporting really favorable results.

During the second 5 years (see tables II and VI) there were 2 more Australian, 2 more Italian and 6 more French reports as well as 2 Czech, 1 English and the first 5 of an amazing group of papers by SCHOU, BAASTRUP and associates. To date SCHOU has authored or co-authored more than 60 publications on lithium.

The third 5 years (see tables III and VI) produced only 15 publications containing new case material. There were 3 reports in the Russian literature but only 1 from the USA (a letter to the editor).

From 1964 until the present (see tables IV and VI) the major clinical psychiatric work on lithium has been centered in Scandinavia and the USA. There will probably be more reports covering more cases during the next 2 years than in the first 2 decades. Demonstration of potential therapeutic usefulness as a prophylactic against recurrent depressions and the prolific, scholarly enthusiasm of SCHOU have been major factors in the growing recognition of lithium's importance.

It would seem logical that if lithium were so specific for manic states that it would also be effective against depressive episodes in the same type patients. CADE tried the treatment for 3 weeks or longer on 3 depressed patients who neither got better nor worse. Most of the early authors also tried treating such patients but the first to report favorable results in 2 cases was MARGULIES in 1955 (who used it in combination with a barbiturate). VOJTĚCHOVSKY in 1957 and ANDREANI in 1958 also reported substantial success. This early work has not been confirmed but it is perhaps worth noting that all three of these investigators used lithium citrate rather than lithium carbonate. HANSEN *et al.* [1959] in a double blind placebo cross-over study with lithium carbonate obtained very inconclusive results. On the other hand, MOSKETI [1963] obtained favorable and rapid results in depressive paranoids utilizing 10% i.v. lithium iodide.

The prophylactic action of lithium was implied almost from the beginning since CADE noted the necessity for continuing the drug in order to prevent relapse. SCHOU gives the credit to BAASTRUP and to HARTIGAN for demonstrating in 6 of 8 patients with recurrent depression that lithium over a 3 year follow-up period was successful as a prophylactic agent. HARTIGAN in turn credits ANDREANI with being the first to note that the drug might 'have to be continued for a very long time' and especially so in recurrent depression. Actually it has been SCHOU himself following the observations of BAASTRUP, later working with him, then alone and then in collaboration with HANSEN, RETBØLL and others, who has brought this fact to wide awareness and demonstrated it most conclusively.

For a period it looked as though production of the material for general medical use would be a real problem. The American College of Neuropsychopharmacology even considered taking out an NDA (New Drug Application) in its own name. There were cries that no American pharmaceutical company would produce the drug because it could not be patented and there would not be any appreciable profit margin. In repudiation of this, not one but two American companies are now preparing to market lithium—Rowell Laboratories, Inc. and Chas. Pfizer & Co., Inc.

The claimed uses of the drug are steadily expanding so that they now include the following conditions:

1. Excitement states regardless of etiology
2. Epilepsy
3. Manic states
4. Psychoses activated by ECT or antidepressant drugs
5. Pre-menstrual tension
6. As prophylaxis against recurrent
   a) manic states
   b) manic-depressive mood swings
   c) recurrent depressions
7. Phobias and obsessive-compulsive behavior.

The mode of action of lithium is currently under intensive investigation and the results will unquestionably provide important insights into the nature, management and prevention of affective disorders.

References

AURELIANUS, CAELIUS: On acute diseases and chronic diseases. DRABKIN, I.E. (ed. and transl.) p. 552 (Chicago University Press, Chicago, Ill. 1950).
Ibid, p. 2.
HENDERSON, D. and GILLESPIE, R.D.: Text-book of psychiatry for students and practitioners: 9th ed., HENDERSON, D. and BATCHELOR, I.R.C. (eds.) (Oxford University Press, London 1962).

Note: For other bibliographic references see 'Bibliography of the Clinical Uses of Lithium in Psychiatry' compiled by NSK and GAK.

Presented at: American Psychiatric Association, Boston, Massachusetts, May 13–17, 1968

Partial support for this research was provided by NIMH, Psychopharmacology Research Branch, Early Clinical Drug Evaluation Unit, Grant No. 13446.

Table 1. New clinical psychiatric cases – The first five years (1949–1953)

Year	Biblio. Number	Author	No. pts.	Manic			Depressed			Prophylactic		
				++	+	o/–	++	+	o/–	++	+	o/–
49	13	CADE	19	10	–	–	–	–	3	on lithium indefinitely		
50	73	ROBERTS[T]	2	–	–	1						
50	4	ASHBURNER	50+	12	–	–				one year plus		
51	65	NOACK and TRAUTNER	100+	29	–	1						
51	20	DESPINOY and de ROMEUF	10	3	–	–			'some'			
51	71	REYSS-BRION and GRAMBERT	12	4	–	1						
52	19	DESCHAMPS and DENIS	8	4	–	–						
53	21	DUC and MAUREL	8	4	–	–						
53	31	GIUSTINO	9	–	–	2						
			218+	66	–	5			3+			

T = toxicity report

Table II. New clinical psychiatric cases – The second five years (1954–1958)

Year	Biblio. Number	Author	No. pts.	Manic ++	Manic +	Manic o/-	Depressed ++	Depressed +	Depressed o/-	Prophylactic ++	Prophylactic +	Prophylactic o/-
'54	14	CARRERE and POCHARD	8	2		-						
'54	33	GLESINGER	104	5	10	6						
'54 '55 '56	94 93 89	SCHOU et al.	153	69	-	16						
'55	56	MARGULIES	4+	N.S.	N.S.	N.S.	2					
'55	96	SIVADON and CHANOIT	23	8	2	-						
'55	18	DAUMEZON et al.	1	1	-	-						
'55	67	OULÈS et al.	13	13	-	-						
'55	100	TEULIÉ et al.	68	16	4	5						
'56	72	RICE	58	14	20	3						
'55 '56 '57	101 29 15	TRAUTNER et al.; GERSHON and TRAUTNER; COATS; TRAUTNER; GERSHON	300+	N.S.	N.S.	N.S.				-	9	1
'56	1	AMISANO	120	108	-	12	8	-		1+		
'57	106	VOJTĚCHOVSKÝ	34	6	3	2			6			
'57	39	HANZLÍČEK	113	16	-	10						
'58	3	ANDREANI et al.	84	10	6	2	10	-	14	'treatment must be continued for a long time'		
			1083+	268	45	56	20	-	20	1+	9	1

N.S. = not stated
T   = toxicity report

Table III. New clinical psychiatric cases – The third five years (1959–1963)

Year	Biblio. Number	Author	No. pts.	Manic ++	Manic +	Manic o/-	Depressed ++	Depressed +	Depressed o/-	Prophylactic ++	Prophylactic +	Prophylactic o/-
'59	83	SCHOU[1]	84+	61	–	11	inconclusive for all 12 patients					
	(38	HANSEN et al.)										
59	10	BELLING	51	18	6	8						
59	12	BOTVINNIKOVA	10	5	5	–						
59	104	VARTANIAN	33	6	–	–						
59	50	KREVELEN and VOORST	1	1	–	–				'prevented cycles'		
60	47	KINGSTONE	17	11	5	1						
61	107	VOORST	1	1	–	–						
61	16	COLBERT	N.S.	N.S.	N.S.	N.S.						
62	45	JOTKOWITZ and GERSHON	1	1[2]	–	–						
62	37	GROMSKA	16	12	4	–						
63	55	MAGGS	28	18	–	10						
63	41	HARTIGAN	45				9	–	1	17	9	11
										(6	–	2)△
63	61	MOSKETTI et al.	127	N.S.	N.S.	N.S.						
63	69	PLOEGSMA	32	8	3	1						
63	70	RAVN and KRAGH	2	N.S.	N.S.	N.S.						
			448+	142	23	31	9	–	1	17	9	11

1 in addition to cases reported during first 5 years. Also includes unpublished study by Hansen.
2 activated by ECT and Tofranil treatment of a depressed patient.
N.S. not stated
△ Recurrent Depressions

Table IV. New clinical psychiatric cases – The fourth five years (1964–1968)

Year	Biblio. Number	Author	No. pts.	Manic ++	Manic +	Manic o/-	Depressed ++	Depressed +	Depressed o/-	Prophylactic ++	Prophylactic +	Prophylactic o/-
'64	63	Nielsen	81	N.S.	N.S.	N.S.						
'64	6	Baastrup	150+							61	11	1
'67	8	Baastrup and Schou								8 (Atypical cases)	7	–
'65	66	Ólafsson	27	17	10	–						
'65	98	Stolt	38	19	3	2[1]						
'65	44	Jacobson	17							17	–	–
'65	105	Verbov et al.[T]	1							'results approach 100%'	–	–
'65	64	Nieto	3	3	–	–				1	–	–
'66	62	Nassr	30	28	–	2						
'66	54	Lindheimer and Schafer	5	5	–	–						
'66	111	Williamson	8	3	–	–	2	–	–	2	–	–
'66	110	Schlagenhauf								36 (manics)	4	5
'66	75	Tupin	110	65	4	5	1	–	5	2 (Recurrent Depressions)	–	5
'68	76	White										
'66	108	Warick	4	3	–	–						
'66	109	Wharton and Fieve	25[2]	11	6	8						
'66	43	Hullin et al.	15	13	–	2						
'66	97	Sletten and Gershon	8							8	–	–

(Baastrup: includes 21 Recurrent Depressions)

Table IV. (Continued)

												Pre-menstrual tension		
66	5	ATTMAN and HAMBERT	1									1	–	5
												7	7	
												manics		
67	59	MELIA	55									1	1	2
												Recurrent Depressions		
67	25	FURLONG and Luby	9	4	1	1								
68	34	GONZALES and LAUTER	69	38	–	1								
68	32	GJESSING	1	18	–	–³								
68	28	GERSHON	N.S.									confirms usefulness		
												N.S.	N.S.	N.S.
68	36	GROF	N.S.									confirms usefulness		
												N.S.	N.S.	N.S.
68	24	Frey	12	N.S.	N.S.	N.S.						confirms usefulness		
68	35	GOTTFRIES	35	27	–	–						N.S.	N.S.	N.S.
68	57	MÅRTENS	4				4	–	–					
68	103	VAADAL	14	5	6	5	2	10	15	20	20	20	20	
68	49	KLINE	238	20	9	5	2	10	15	20	(30			12)⁴
			960+	279+	39+	25+	9+	10	20		174	50	30

1 = 24 episodes in 16 patients
2 = 25 episodes in 19 patients
3 = on lithium only
4 = for patients on medication 1 year or longer
N.S. = not stated
T = toxicity report

Table V. New psychiatric cases: overall total

	No. of Papers	No. pts.	Manic ++	Manic +	Manic o/-	Depressed ++	Depressed +	Depressed o/-	Prophylactic ++	Prophylactic +	Prophylactic o/-
1949–1953	9	218+	66	–	5			3+			
1954–1958	16	1083+	268	45	56	20	–	20	1+	9	1
1959–1963	15	448+	142	23	31	9	–	1	17	9	11
1964–1968	30	960+	279+	39+	25+	9+	10	20	174	50	30
Total	70	2709+	755+	107+	117+	38+	10	44+	192+	68	42
%			77%	11%	12%	41%	11%	48%	63%	23%	14%

Table VI.

Year	Biblio. Number	Author	Subject
'53	40	HARANT et al.	Calcium, sodium and lithium metabolism
53	52	LAFON et al.	Review
54	68	PLICHET	Review
54	11	BLANDIN	Discussion
55	22	(unsigned)	Editorial in Lancet
55	101	TRAUTNER et al.	Excretion, retention and ionic balance
57	2	ANDREANI	Electrocardiograms
57	77	SCHOU	Biology and pharmacology of lithium ion
58	86	SCHOU	Toxicity
58	87	SCHOU	Renal elimination
58	88	SCHOU	Distribution between serum and tissues
58	46	KAPPLINGHAUS	Review
59	81	SCHOU	Review
59	91	SCHOU	Therapeutic and toxic properties
60	82	SCHOU	Review
60	85	SCHOU	Review
60	30	GERSHON and YUWILER	Review
61	112	WINGARD	Letter to JAMA editor
62	60	MESSINA and VECCHI	Pharmacology and toxicology
62	95	SHAIUSUPOVA	Review
63	78	SCHOU	EKG
63	90	SCHOU	Review
64	74	ROTH	Review
64	99	STROMGREN and SCHOU	Review
64	79	SCHOU	Review
64	42	HERTRICH	Review
65	53	LANG	Lab measurement
65	23	EPSTEIN et al.	Urinary excretion in mania
65	17	COPPEN et al.	Electrolyte distribution
66	9	BAKER and WINOKUR	Cerebrospinal fluid
66	51	KOLB	Discussion
66	26	GARTSIDE et al.	Evoked cortical somatosensory response
66	58	MAYFIELD and BROWN	Electroencephalogram
67	92	SCHOU and BAASTRUP	Dosage and control
67	80	SCHOU	Review
67	84	SCHOU	Review
67	7	BAASTRUP and SCHOU	Review
68	27	GERSHON	Review
68	48	KLINE	History of psychiatric usage

		Non-human	
58	102	TRAUTNER et al.	Effect on pregnancy in rats

Bibliography of the Clinical Uses of Lithium in Psychiatry

compiled by
NATHAN S. KLINE, M.D.
GLORIA A. KISTNER

1. AMISANO, A.: Tesi di specializzazione. Neuropsychiatria, Modena Anno Acc., 1955–1956.
2. ANDREANI, G.: Rilievi elettrocardiografici durante il trattamento di malattie mentali con sali di litio. G. Clin. med. *38:* 1759–1775 (1957).
3. ANDREANI, G.; CASELLI, G. e MARTELLI, G.: Rilievi clinici ed elettroencefalografici durante il trattamento con sali di litio in malati psichiatrici. G. Psichiat. Neuropat. *86:* 273–328 (1958).
4. ASHBURNER, J.V.: Correspondence – A case of chronic mania treated with lithium citrate and terminating fatally. Méd. J. Austr. *2:* 386 (1950).
5. ATTMAN, P.O. and HAMBERT, G.: Lithiumbehandling på atypisk indikation. Läkartidningen *63:* 4674–4675 (1966).
6. BAASTRUP, P.C.: The use of lithium in manic-depressive psychosis. Comprehens. Psychiat. *5:* 396–408 (1964).
7. BAASTRUP, P.C. and SCHOU, M.: Kemisk Psykoseprofylakse Lithium mod Maniodepressiv Psykose. Nord. Med. *77:* 180–187 (1967).
8. BAASTRUP, P.C. and SCHOU, M.: Lithium as a prophylactic agent. Its effect against recurrent depressions and manic-depressive psychosis. Arch. gen. Psychiat. *16:* 162–172 (1967).
9. BAKER, M.A. and WINOKUR, G.: Cerebrospinal fluid lithium in manic illness. Brit. J. Psychiat. *112:* 163–165 (1966).
10. BELLING, G.: Lithiumbehandling pa et sindssyge hospital. Ugeskr. Laeg. *121:* 1193–1195 (1959).
11. BLANDIN, M.P.: Discussion. Ann. méd.-psychol. *112:* 572 (1954).
12. BOTVINNIKOVA, M.I.: Lithium salts in the treatment of maniacal states of different origin and of certain mental disorders associated with organic diseases of the brain. Zh. Nevropat. Psikhiat. *59:* 1222–1223 (1959).
13. CADE, J.F.J.: Lithium salts in the treatment of psychotic excitement. Med. J. Austr. *2:* 349–352 (1949).
14. CARRERE, M.J. et POCHARD, MLLE.: Le citrate de Lithium dans le traitement des syndromes d'excitation psychomotrice. Ann. méd. psychol. *112:* 566–572 (1954).
15. COATS, D.A.; TRAUTNER, E.M. and GERSHON, S.: The treatment of Lithium poisoning. Austr. Ann. Med. *6:* 11–15 (1957).
16. COLBERT, E.G.: In letters to the editor: Lithium salts. J. amer. Ass. *176:* 744 (1961).
17. COPPEN, A.; MALLESON, A. and SHAW, D.M.: Effects of lithium carbonate on electrolyte distribution in man. Lancet *I:* 682–683 (1965).

18.   DAUMEZON, G.; GUIBERT, M. et CHANOIT, P.: Un cas d'intoxication grave par le Lithium. Ann. méd.-psychol. *113:* 673–679 (1955).

19.   DESCHAMPS et DENIS: Premiers résultats du traitement des états d'excitation maniaque par les sels de Lithium. L'avenir méd. Lyon *49:* 152–157 (1952).

20.   DESPINOY et ROMEUF DE: Emploi des sels de Lithium en thérapeutique psychiatrique. Congrès des Médecine Alienistes et Neurologistes de France, 49th Session, p. 509–515 (1951).

21.   DUC, N. et MAUREL, H.: Le traitement des états d'agitation psycho-motrice par le Lithium. Le concours médical *75:* 1817–1820 (1953).

22.   (Editorial) Lithium Salts in Manic Psychosis. Lancet *I:* 854–855 (1955).

23.   EPSTEIN, R.; GRANT, L.; HERJANIC, M. and WINOKUR, G.: Urinary excretion of Lithium in mania. J. amer. med. Ass. *192:* 409 (1965).

24.   FREY, T.: Discussion. Nord. psykiat. T. *20:* 465 (1966).

25.   FURLONG, F.W. and LUBY, E.D.: Lithium in the control of mania. Int. J. Neuropsychiat. *3:* 348–353 (1967).

26.   GARTSIDE, I.B.; LIPPOLD, O.C.J. and MELDRUM, B.S.: The evoked cortical somatosensory response in normal man and its modification by oral lithium carbonate. Electroenceph. clin. Neurophysiol. *20:* 382–390 (1966).

27.   GERSHON, S.: Use of Lithium salts in psychiatric disorders. Dis. nerv. Syst. *29:* 51–55 (1968).

28.   GERSHON, S.: The possible thymoleptic effect of the lithium ion. Amer. J. Psychiat. *124:* 1452–1456 (1968).

29.   GERSHON, S. and TRAUTNER, E.M.: The treatment of shock-dependency by pharmacological agents. Med. J. Austr. *43:* 783–787 (1956).

30.   GERSHON, S. and YUWILER, A.: Lihtium Ion: A specific psychopharmacological approach to the treatment of mania. J. Neuropsychiat. *1:* 229–241 (1960).

31.   GIUSTINO, P.: Il citrato di litio nel trattamento degli stati di eccitazione psicotica. Riv. Psichiat. (Pesaro) *79:* 307–311 (1953).

32.   GJESSING, L.R.: Lithium citrate loading of a patient with periodic catatonia. Acta psychiat. scand. *43:* 372–375 (1967).

33.   GLESINGER, B.: Evaluation of Lithium in treatment of psychotic excitement. Med. J. Austr. *41:* 277–283 (1954).

34.   GONZALES, R. und LAUTER, H.: Zur Therapie manisch-depressiver Psychosen mit Lithium Salzen. Nervenarzt *39:* 11–16 (1968).

35.   GOTTFRIES, C.G.: Discussion. Nord. psykiat. T. *20:* 466 (1966).

36.   GROF, P.: Preliminary experiences with the prophylactic use of Lithium against recurrent endogenous depressions. Paper read at the 'I. Zentraleuropäische Pharmakopsychiatrische Symposium', October 1967.

37.   GROMSKA, J.: Leczenie stanow maniakalnych solami litu. Neurol. Neurochir. Psychiat. pol. *12:* 575–581 (1962).

38.   HANSEN, C.J.; RETBOLL, J. and SCHOU, M.: Unpublished study (1958). Described in SCHOU, M.: Lithium in psychiatric therapy. Stock taking after ten years. Psychopharmacologia *1:* 65–78 (1959).

39.   HANZLIČEK, L.: Lithiové soli v psychiatrii. In Problémy psychiatrie v. praxi a ve výzkuma; memorial volume to the 75th birthday anniversary of Prof. Dr. Z. Mysliveček. Czechoslovak Medical Press, 1957.

40.   HARANT, H.; DUC, N.; CARON et MAUREL, H.: Remarques sur la pharmacologie du Lithium. Presse méd. *61:* 713 (1953).

41.   HARTIGAN, G.P.: The use of Lithium salts in affective disorders. Brit. J. Psychiat. *109:* 810–814 (1963).

42.   HERTRICH, O.: Differentialindikationen für psychosenspezifische Psychopharmaka.

In BRADLEY, P.B.; FLÜGEL, F. und HOCH, P. (Ed.) Neuropsychopharmacology *3:* 391–393 (Elsevier, Amsterdam/London/New York 1964).

43.   HULLIN, R.P.; MCDONALD, R. and DRANSFIELD, G.A.: Metabolic balance studies on the effect of Lithium salts in manic-depressive psychosis. Excerpta med. Int. Congr. Series No. *117:* 235–236 (1966).

44.   JACOBSON, J.E.: The hypomanic alert: A program designed for greater therapeutic control. Amer. J. Psychiat. *122:* 295–299 (1965).

45.   JOTKOWITZ, M.W. and GERSHON, S.: Manic reactions following combined 'Tofranil' (Imipramine) and electroconvulsive therapy. Med. J. Austr. *49:* 87–90 (1962).

46.   KAPPLINGHAUS, R.: Lithium-Behandlung in der Psychiatrie. Med. Kli. *53:* 660–661 (1958).

47.   KINGSTONE, E.: The Lithium treatment of hypomanic and manic states. Comprehens. Psychiat. *1:* 317–320 (1960).

48.   KLINE, N.S.: The history of Lithium usage in psychiatry (submitted for publication).

49.   KLINE, N.S.; MASON, B.; SWENSON, J. and WINICK, L.: Lithium usage in ambulatory psychiatric patients (submitted for publication).

50.   KREVELEN, VON, D.A. und VOORST, VAN, J.A.: Lithium in der Behandlung einer Psychose unklarer Genese bei einem Jugendlichen. Z. Kinderpsychiat. *26:* 148–152 (1959).

51.   KOLB, L.: Discussion. Amer. J. Psychiat. *123:* 206–207 (1966).

52.   LAFON, R.; DUC, N. et MAUREL, H.: Traitement des états d'excitation psycho-motrice par le carbonate de Lithium. Presse méd. *61:* 713 (1953).

53.   LANG, W. und HERRMANN, R.: Eine Methode zur Flammenspektrophotometrischen Lithiumbestimmung in Serum. Z. ges. exp. Med. *139:* 200–212 (1965).

54.   LINDHEIMER, J.W. and SCHAFER, D.W.: Lithium treatment for mania. Diseases of the nervous system *27:* 122–126 (1966).

55.   MAGGS, R.: Treatment of manic illness with Lithium carbonate. Brit. J. Psychiat. *109:* 56–65 (1963).

56.   MARGULIES, M.: Suggestions for the treatment of schizophrenic and manic-depressive patients. Med. J. Austr. *1:* 137–143 (1955).

57.   MÅRTENS, S.: Discussion. Nord. psykiat. T. *20:* 465 (1966).

58.   MAYFIELD, D. and BROWN, R.G.: The clinical laboratory and electroencephalographic effects of Lithium. J. Psychiat. Res. *4:* 207–219 (1966).

59.   MELIA, P.I.: A pilot trial of Lithium carbonate in recurrent affective disorders. J. Irish med. Ass. *60:* 160–170 (1967).

60.   MESSINA, B. e VECCHI, L.: Problemi attuali inerenti alla somministrazione dei sali di litio. Clinica Terapeutica *22:* 940–951 (1962).

61.   MOSKETI, K.V.; BELSKAIA, G.M. and MURATOVA, I.D.: Experience in the use of iodinated Lithium in the treatment of some psychotic states. Zh. Nevropat. Psikhiat. *63:* 92–95 (1963).

62.   NASSR, D.G.: Observations on the use of Lithium carbonate in psychiatry. Int. J. Neuropsychiat. *2:* 160–165 (1966).

63.   NIELSEN, J.: Magnesium – Lithium studies 1. Serum and erythrocyte magnesium in patients with manic states during Lithium treatment. Acta psychiat. scand. *40:* 190–196 (1964).

64.   NIETO, D.: Tratamiento de los estados maniacos con carbonato de litio. Rev. Invest. clin. (Guadalajara) *4:* 81–84 (1965).

65.   NOACK, C.H. and TRAUTNER, E.M.: The Lithium treatment of maniacal psychosis. Med. J. Austr. *2:* 219–222 (1951).

66.   ÓLAFSSON, O.: Lithium medferd vid psychosis manio-depressiva. Laeknabladid *50:* 51–55 (1965).

67.   OULÈS, J.; SOUBRIÉ, R. et SALLES, P.: A propos du traitement des crises de manie par les sels de Lithium. Congrès des Médecins Alienistes et Neurologistes de France. *53:* 570–573 (1955).

68.   PLICHET, A.: Le traitement des états maniaques par les sels de Lithium. Presse méd. *62:* 869–871 (1954).

69.   PLOEGSMA, W.: Behandeling van psychotische opwindingstoestanden met Lithii carbonas. Ned. T. Geneesk. *107:* 397–402 (1963).

70.   RAVN, J. und KRAGH, E.R.: Behandlung manischer Patienten mit Chlorprothixen (Truxal®) im Vergleich mit anderen Behandlungsmethoden, besonders mit Hinblick auf die Dauer der Zeit der Stationierung. Acta Psychiat. scand. *39:* Suppl. *169:* 139–151 (1963).

71.   REYSS-BRION, R. et GRAMBERT, J.: Essai de traitement des états d'excitation psychotique par le citrate de Lithium. J. méd. Lyon *32:* 985–989 (1951).

72.   RICE, D.: The use of Lithium salts in the treatment of manic states. J. ment. Sci. *102:* 604–611 (1956).

73.   ROBERTS, E.L.: A case of chronic mania treated with Lithium citrate and terminating fatally. Med. J. Austr. *2:* 261–262 (1950).

74.   ROTH, M.: Depressive and manic psychoses and allied disorders. Curr. Med. Drugs. *4:* 3–18 (1964).

75.   SCHLAGENHAUF, G.; TUPIN, J. and WHITE, R.B.: The use of Lithium carbonate in the treatment of manic psychoses. Amer. J. Psychiat. *123:* 201–206 (1966).

76.   SCHLAGENHAUF, G.; TUPIN, J. and WHITE, R.B.: Three years experience with Lithium carbonate (submitted for publication, 1968).

77.   SCHOU, M.: Biology and pharmacology of the Lithium Ion. Pharmacol. Rev. *9:* 17–58 (1957).

78.   SCHOU, M.: Electrocardiographic changes during treatment with Lithium and with drugs of the Imipramine-type. Acta Psychiat. scand. *39:* Suppl. *169:* 258–259 (1963).

79.   SCHOU, M.: General Discussion. In BRADLEY, P.B.; FLÜGEL, F. and HOCH, P. (eds.) Neuropsychopharmacology Vol. *3:* (Elsevier, Amsterdam/London/New York 1964).

80.   SCHOU, M.: Lithium: Ein Spezificum gegen manisch-depressive Psychose. Arzneimittelforsch. *17:* 172–176 (1967).

81.   SCHOU, M.: Lithium i den psykiatriske terapi. Bibl. Laeger *151:* 121–147 (1959).

82.   SCHOU, M.: Lithium in psychiatric therapy. Danish med. Bull. *7:* 32 (1960).

83.   SCHOU, M.: Lithium in psychiatric therapy. Stock-taking after ten years. Psychopharmacologia *1:* 65–78 (1959).

84.   SCHOU, M.: Lithium in psychiatry – A review. In EFRON, D.; COLE, J.; LEVINE, J. and WITTENBORN, J.R. (eds.) Psychopharmacology. A review of progress. Presented at ACNP meeting, December 1967.

85.   SCHOU, M.: Lithium som laegemiddel. Arch. Pharmaci Chemi *67:* 177–184 (1960).

86.   SCHOU, M.: Lithium studies. 1. Toxicity. Acta pharmacolo. *15:* 70–84 (1958).

87.   SCHOU, M.: Lithium studies. 2. Renal elimination. Acta Pharmacol. *15:* 85–98 (1958).

88.   SCHOU, M.: Lithium studies. 3. Distribution between serum and tissues. Acta Pharmacol. *15:* 115–124 (1958).

89.   SCHOU, M.: Lithiumterapi ved mani. Nord. Med. *55:* 790–794 (1956).

90.   SCHOU, M.: Normothymotics, 'Mood-Normalizers'. Are lithium and the Imipramine drugs specific for affective disorders? Brit. J. Psychiat. *109:* 803–809 (1963).

91.   SCHOU, M.: Therapeutic and toxic properties of Lithium. Acta Psychiat. scand. *34:* Suppl. *136:* 51–54 (1959).

92.   SCHOU, M. and BAASTRUP, P.C.: Lithium treatment of manic-depressive disorder, dosage and control. J. amer. med. Ass. *201:* 696–699 (1967).

93.   SCHOU, M.; JUEL-NIELSEN, N.; STRÖMGREN, E. and VOLDBY, H.: Behandling af maniske psykoser med lithium. Ugeskr. Laeg. *117:* 93–101 (1955).

94.   SCHOU, M.; JUEL-NIELSEN, N.; STRÖMGREN, E. and VOLDBY, H.: The treatment of manic psychoses by the administration of Lithium salts. J. Neurol. Neurosurg. Psychiat. *17:* 250–260 (1954).

95.   SHAIUSUPOVA, A.U.: Treatment of manic conditions with Lithium salts. Meditsinskii Zhurnal Ubekistana. *11:* 36–37 (1962).

96.   SIVADON, P. et CHANOIT, P.: L'Emploi du Lithium dans l'agitation psychomotrice a propos d'une expérience clinique. Ann. méd.-psychol. *113:* 790–796 (1955).

97.   SLETTEN, I.W. and GERSHON, S.: The premenstrual syndrome: a discussion of its pathophysiology and treatment with Lithium Ion. Comprehens. Psychiat. *7:* 197–206 (1966).

98.   STOLT, G.: Behandling med litiumsalter vid mano-depressiva stämningstillstånd. Läkartidningen *62:* 3018–3024 (1965).

99.   STRÖMGREN, E. and SCHOU, M.: Lithium treatment of manic states. Postgrad. med. J. *35:* 83–86 (1964).

100.   TEULIÉ, M.; FOLLIN et BÉGOIN: Etude de l'action des sels de Lithium dans états d'excitation psycho-motrice. Encéphale. *44:* 266–285 (1955).

101.   TRAUTNER, E.M.; MORRIS, R.; NOACK, C.H. and GERSHON, S.: The excretion and retention of ingested Lithium and its effect on the ionic balance of man. Med. J. Austr. *2:* 280–291 (1955).

102.   TRAUTNER, E.M.; PENNYCUIK, P.R.; MORRIS, R.J.H.; GERSHON, S. and SHANKLY, K.H.: The effects of prolonged sub-toxic Lithium ingestion on pregnancy in rats. Austr. J. Exp. Biol. med. Sci. *36:* 305–321 (1958).

103.   VAADAL, J.: Discussion. Nord. psykiat. T. *20:* 458–462 (1966).

104.   VARTANIAN, M.E.: Result of Lithium carbonate therapy in agitation states. Zh. Nevropat. Psikhiat. *59:* 586–589 (1959).

105.   VERBOV, J.L.; PHILLIPS, J.D. and FIFE, D.G.: A case of Lithium intoxication. Postgrad. med. J. *41:* 190–192 (1965).

106.   VOJTĚCHOVSKÝ, M.: Zkušenosti s Léčbou solemi Lithia. Problémy psychiatrie v praxi a ve zýzkuma; memorial volume to the 75th birthday anniversary of Prof. Z. Myslivecek (Czechoslovak Medical Press, 1957).

107.   VOORST, VAN, J.A.: Behandeling van een lijder aan manie met Lithiumcarbonaat. Ned. T. Geneesk. *105:* 323–325 (1961).

108.   WARICK, L.H.: Lithium salts in treatment of manic states. Dis. nerv. Syst. *27:* 527–530 (1966).

109.   WHARTON, R.N. and FIEVE, R.R.: The use of Lithium in the affective psychoses. Amer. J. Psychiat. *123:* 706–712 (1966).

110.   WHITE, R.B.; SCHLAGENHAUF, G. and TUPIN, J.P.: The treatment of manic depressive states with Lithium carbonate. Curr. psychiat. Ther. *6:* 230–242 (1966).

111.   WILLIAMSON, B.: Psychiatry since Lithium. Dis. nerv. Syst. *27:* 775–782 (1966).

112.   WINGARD, C.: Letter to the editor: Lithium salts. J. amer. med. Ass. *175:* 340 (1961).

Partial support for this investigation was provided by the Early Clinical Drug Evaluation Unit, Psychopharmacology Research Branch, NIMH, Grant No. MH 13446.